THE 9 KEY TECHNIQUES FOR RAISING RESPECTFUL CHILDREN WHO MAKE RESPONSIBLE CHOICES

The Dr. Karen Parenting Philosophy

By Karen Bailes Ruskin, PsyD, LMFT

Copyright © 2009 by **Karen Bailes Ruskin, PsyD, LMFT**

ISBN: 978-0-578-03270-2

AUTHOR'S NOTE

Over the last sixteen years I have seen many clients in my practice, in addition to interacting with people in additional contexts. I have drawn on their stories in order to illustrate the experiences I describe in this book. I have invented all the names and identifying data used in the stories, which are composites. Any resulting resemblance to persons either living or dead is entirely unintentional and coincidental.

Thank you to my loving husband, Seth, for all of your support of my personal growth and professional endeavors. Thank you, honey, for being such a wonderful husband to me, and father to our son. Your style of interaction leads us to feel loved, honored, valued, respected, special, and appreciated each day.

Thank you to my precious son, Jeremy, for being the person that you are every day. Thank you for your love, your personality, for being who you are. I feel so blessed to have you as my son.

Thank you to my dear mother and father, Vivian and Neil, for being parents that have always interacted with me in a style that has led me to feel loved, valued, and respected. Your methods of parenting allowed me to always feel capable to do whatever I put my mind to. I am so proud to be your daughter.

Thank you to my brother, Mike, for being a loving and responsible older brother and contributing in a very significant way in my development of self-worth and understanding males during my youth.

Thank you to my grandparents, Gertrude and Ben, Rae and Al. Although you are long gone, I know that without the role you played in parenting my parents, they would not be the parents they have been and are.

CONTENTS

INTRODUCTION

This book is for parents who are raising children of any age. If you have children, or plan on having children, it is important that you are consciously aware of your parenting philosophy. The benefits of incorporating the Dr. Karen Parenting Philosophy, along with the nine techniques that support it, has been proven successful time and time again.

For the past sixteen years, my clinical work with individuals, couples, and families has informed my theoretical view. My educational background has also played a significant role in creating my philosophy, as have my experiences within my own family dynamic, and my observations through the years of friends and extended family.

The parenting education workshop that I developed and teach brings such positive shifts in the families of the parents who have attended that I decided to put my philosophy and techniques together in book form. I believe it is my duty to spread this knowledge to those whose lives I may normally not have an opportunity to help.

My passionate belief about child rearing is one I have taught to many parents. I have helped them incorporate nine techniques into their family life with consistency. Parents report their appreciation for this knowledge, and tell me that it has significantly and positively impacted their family dynamic. I always feel genuine excitement and am happy when the contributions I make lead others to a better place than they were in before they were introduced to my parenting philosophy and nine techniques. In the book *Steps to an Ecology of Mind*, Gregory Bateson defines information as "a difference which makes a difference" (p. 453). Perhaps the information this book can provide you can be a difference which makes a difference for you and those you love.

When children are respectful and make responsible choices, it makes for a happier child. When they become adults, respectfulness also significantly impacts the family dynamic in a positive way. My expertise lies in viewing a presenting problem in a systemic way and then developing solutions that positively impact the person presenting the problem, as well as the other members of that family unit. To help a family develop a sense of harmony and peace instead of war is indeed wonderful.

When children are respectful and responsible, they feel good about who they are as individuals. This further influences how others relate to them, how they relate to others, and so on. When children are respectful and make responsible choices, this also affects the types of experiences they will have every moment of every day. A child's understanding of himself, how he relates to others, how others relate to him, and the experiences that he has all directly affect who this child becomes, this child's sense of self, and the life this child will lead as an adult. People often ask me if I practice what I preach. The answer is, *how could I not do so?*

Raising our children is a most rewarding, fulfilling,

exciting, challenging, and at times painstaking experience. *Having children means that it is our job, our duty, and our responsibility to help our children to help themselves develop a character that is respectful to himself and others, and to make responsible choices.* It saddens me to see so many parents who have lost this belief along the way. When a child is respectful and making responsible choices and that behavior feels right, then we see a child who at his core is respectful and responsible. That is the child we are trying to help develop. The child that is respectful and responsible is the child that feels good about himself.

Whose responsibility is it to help our children develop this sense of who they are if not the parents? I say this, but I am all too aware that not all parents hold this view as their own. There are parents who pride themselves that their children are disrespectful just as long as no one is being disrespectful to their children. It makes the parents feel like their children are holding their own and in charge. I suggest that we help our children be leaders who others follow because they respect our children, not fear them. There are also parents who time and time again show that whether it is their child or another who is behaving disrespectfully, there is an acceptance by the adult that the disrespectful behavior is expected. A parent who has a "girls will be girls" or "boys will be boys" attitude with regard to disrespectful behavior is a parent who accepts the negative without any expectations of the positive. In my opinion, that is disgraceful. As adults, we should expect respect and responsible actions.

Simply demanding responsible and respectful behavior does not work. Teaching such behavior through the style we use to interact with our children does work. They learn to have those expectations of themselves and others. Disrespectful and irresponsible behavior has no connection to our race, religion, age, financial status, or gender. It is what we do as parents that plays a significant and undeniable role in who our children grow up to be.

Raising children to be respectful and make responsible choices may sometimes be difficult, or even completely exasperating. When our children are being disrespectful, even the most mild-mannered of parents can fall into downright adult temper tantrums. When our children make irresponsible choices, this can also be very challenging for parents. The parents' reaction may depend on the age of the child, how extreme the irresponsible and/or disrespectful behavior is, the parents' personality, and the history of the behavior of the child.

This book is not about discipline. Far from it. Nor is my intent to help you instill fear in your children that they have to listen to you and be respectful just because you are telling them to, and/or just because you are the parent. My intent is to help you help your children develop into respectful human beings who make responsible choices, thereby becoming respectful and responsible adults. Wouldn't it be lovely if all parents chose right now to actively take part in this journey of helping their children become responsible and respectful?

For some of you, the philosophy and ideas presented in this book will validate and support the parenting philosophy you already have. These techniques may reinforce the concepts upon which you rear your children. In essence, the Dr. Karen Parenting Philosophy's nine techniques can help provide you with a way to verbalize what you already do. The techniques in this book will help you to enhance, clarify, and expand your parenting style.

For others, the Dr. Karen Parenting Philosophy and the nine techniques will be new and different, perhaps even contrary to your current understanding of child rearing. Some parents may feel that they have tried everything with no success. You may find my ideas exciting and refreshing, perhaps even life saving, when nothing else seems to have worked.

Others may be in the early stages of child rearing and have not yet settled on a parenting philosophy. Thus, wanting information on raising children is your desire.

It is possible that you may find my philosophy and techniques questionable, even appalling. If so, you may find other literature that suggests child-rearing practices from a different angle.

Whatever your purpose of reading this book may be, and whatever your current parenting philosophy is, know that I have seen my philosophy of child rearing help make positive shifts in the lives of many, time and time again. Of course, there are no guarantees in life; it is your choice whether you want to try out what this book has to offer.

Let me share a story about a very skeptical man who attended one of my parenting education workshops. Within the first three minutes of my workshop, this man questioned the validity of what I taught. I told him that I consistently hear from parents who incorporate my view and they do find improvement and true positive shifts, although, of course, there are no guarantees.

After the workshop, this man came up to me and asked how my ideas could possibly work. He was extremely doubtful and critical; in fact he was quite argumentative. But he also said he had enjoyed the presentation. Since I was so enthusiastic about my belief and he was at a loss regarding what else he could do with children that were so disrespectful, and that they typically made irresponsible choices, he said he was going to at least try my ideas. The next day, I received a long e-mail from him about why my ideas could not work, but once again he stated that he would try them, anyway. Approximately two days later, I received another e-mail from him. This time, he said that he thought my ideas might be workable. He had been trying them and thought he saw some positive changes. He wanted to let me know that he could not believe how quickly incorporating the ideas had changed his children's behaviors. A few days later, he e-mailed me again and said my ideas were truly helping his family. He added that he was quite surprised.

Two weeks after that, he e-mailed me again. This time, he said my philosophy and techniques had helped him and his family. Three months later, he followed up with another e-mail explaining he loved my philosophy and techniques. He reported on the huge change in his children and how he now related to them and how they now related to him. Several months after, he sent me another e-mail in which he wrote that my philosophy and techniques are *the key* to child rearing. Almost a year later, he followed up again, stating that the positive effects continued. He thanked me sincerely. This story is a lovely example that the techniques can work even for those that are skeptics.

As you open your mind to a very exciting parenting approach, I wish you the best. I believe in my philosophy with all sincerity in my heart and my mind. There have been times when people have questioned my philosophy, but the Dr. Karen Parenting Philosophy and the techniques always shine through. I have seen and continue to see how my philosophy and techniques work, even in the most challenging situations. I wish you the best as you read this book and incorporate what you read into your own life.

CHAPTER 1

BEING RESPECTFUL AND RESPONSIBLE: WHAT DOES THAT REALLY MEAN? PARENTS AS EDUCATORS

Picture a five-year-old child calling his friend a butt-head. Is that statement about his friend positive or negative? It is clearly negative, and perhaps the friend feels hurt. Is the statement respectful? Is it fun? Does it feel good for either child? Is there any possible positive in this statement? Picture another scenario: a four-year-old is running in the house with her friend. Both children are giggling and having fun. This is not a competition; they are enjoying their togetherness. Then one of the girls says, "You are such a slow-poke, I can beat you every time." She giggles, runs, and says it again. You observe this sequence for a third time. The play has now shifted from two children having fun to one child being disrespectful to the other, and that child being hurt. Playing has gone from "team running" to "competitive racing." In and of itself, competition is not harmful. Competition can be healthy. The problem is the verbal message one child sends to the other. One girl was not being very sportsman-like.

When you hear your child making unsportsmanlike, negative statements and decide to "let them work it out", this is making a poor choice. It may be hard at times to decide when to intervene and when to let them work it out. When it comes to the topic of respect, however, it is important to always intervene and educate a young child as to why it is not kind and not respectful to speak to a friend that way. Children are continuously developing their sense of character. This learning informs their future choices, their sense of self, and their character.

Being respectful to others means being kind, considerate, thoughtful, and compassionate. Being respectful means caring about another's well-being, and not wanting to actively do or say anything to be hurtful to their sense of self and well-being. Being hurtful or unkind is not only disrespectful, it is also being irresponsible, and making an irresponsible choice says something negative about you.

Picture your fifteen-year-old son coming home from school with a female classmate to study for an exam together. You go into the kitchen, where they are studying to get a glass of water, and happen to overhear your son laugh and say, "Joe is such a big, fat pig. With that retarded lisp he's got, there ain't no girl who would do him, even if she was paid to." Are you horrified to hear this? To hear your own child speak in such a vulgar manner is painful. You are in a tough place now. If you say something at that point, it will embarrass your son. But we must teach our children respectful and responsible behavior. So what do you do?

When it comes to kids, sometimes you can - and should - say something right then and there, when the behavior is happening. Other times, it is best to wait for when you are alone with your child. It is not always easy to make the decision if or when to say something, and occasionally it is best not to say anything. What do you think? Is this one of those times?

Remember your goal. If you are dealing with very young children, four or five years old, for example, not only do you want to teach what being respectful is to help your child learn in terms of character development, but you are also trying to help in the here and now. With a teenager, it is imperative to teach him. As a parent, you want your words to be heard and to have long-term impact. Considering your child's development is an important issue in helping you decide what to say and when to say it. With teenagers, what their friends think of them is so important that if you tried to say something in that moment, your teen may see it as a put-down. For self-preservation, he might come back at you in a nasty way and engage in a power-struggle, as he is dealing with independence-dependence issues. He may not hear or absorb your words, either here and now, or in the future. You should not infer that you should never talk to your teen in front of his friends. On the contrary, there are many occasions where you can speak to your teen in front of his friends. But you should evaluate whether your teen will actually hear you when you speak.

Going back to the example of the teenage boy, you want to help your teenager understand that talking negatively about another lowers the speaker himself. The teenager who speaks in a disrespectful manner about another person shows that he is lacking sensitivity and compassion. It is best in this case to talk with your teenager after his friend has left. Discuss with him how challenging it must be to live the way the boy with the lisp does, and how he must feel. Help your son understand that to express his opinions is good, but he needs to show respect and intelligence while he is making his point. For an example, you can discuss alternatives with your son. You can suggest that he can still express his opinions to his female friend, but he should do so in a different manner. He can, for example, say, "It must be hard for Joe, being so overweight and having a lisp, to be able to spend time with smart, beautiful women." Tell your son he can say, "Man, I feel lucky to be who I am. I have all these rockin' qualities and I'm getting to spend time with you." You can explain to your son that this statement makes the girl feel special because it shows he views himself positively, he views her positively, and he still made his point about what Joe does not have, though now in a thoughtful manner that shows compassion rather than disrespect.

Be aware of your child's stage of development and personality as you make decisions about what to say and when to say it. This will help your children learn to be respectful and make responsible choices.

I have often heard parents either imply or directly say, "I don't want to be the hovering parent. Sometimes it's important for kids to work things out on their own." Yes, it is important for kids to experience self-learning. Sometimes, it is very important for them to work things out on their own. But be aware that without your teaching them what being respectful is, they may not learn. Being actively involved in your child's development of his core value system and character is not hovering.

Without your help, children may not learn to make responsible decisions about being thoughtful concerning themselves or others. Of course, some children do learn respectful and responsible behavior, even when you don't teach it directly. You can certainly increase the odds by giving them opportunities to learn. If you believe that negative statements are just made "in good fun," then you might ask yourself these questions: Where does good fun begin and where does it end? Who defines good fun? Is it the person making the comment? The target of the comment? If you see disrespectful behavior as good fun, then don't be surprised when your child displays disrespectful behavior toward you. For an example, if your child says, "Mom, you suck at cooking," are you okay with that? Is it a respectful comment? What if your child says, "Grandma is so old, she's on her way out the door, anyway. Why bother visiting her?" Do you think it is okay to say such a thing? If you say yes, then you have a problem. Yes, your child is entitled to his opinions, but *how he expresses them* is extremely important. The words he chooses mark the difference between disrespectful and respectful, between irresponsible and responsible.

Not all parents choose to help their children make responsible choices, and accept certain behaviors as acceptable. You can see this in toddlers when one boy grabs a toy from another boy, the boy's mother just says, "Well, boys will be boys," or, "Let them work it out." There are also lazy parents and parents that are so self-absorbed that they pay scant attention to their children. Such parents feel it is just too much work and takes too much of their energy to help their kids learn to be respectful and responsible. Although the toddler and preschool years are the prime time to teach your child respectful techniques he can use to work out situations, it is never too late. It is this education that absolutely will impact your child's choices now and in the future.

For an example, consider the eleven-year-old girl who tells her eight-year-old stepsister, "I hate you! And if you tell your mom, I'll kill you." When the mother notices that her biological daughter (the younger sister) is displaying symptoms of depression, perhaps she does not sit down with her and ask detailed questions about how she feels about living in a blended family. Perhaps she does not sit down with the father of her stepchild to discuss his take on things. Perhaps she just says to her young daughter, "Stop with the sour puss." Perhaps she just thinks it is a stage and says nothing. This is lazy parenting. Not talking to your kid about her feelings is lazy parenting. Lazy parenting is not knowing how your kid is feeling because you are not taking the time to really communicate with her.

In this example, the eight-year-old does not feel she is being treated as an important member of the family. Specifically, her sadness is not taken seriously. She is being told to, basically, "suck it up." Because of her home environment, she does not learn to make responsible choices outside her home. She develops a "suck-it-up" philosophy. She develops into a child that feels she, and others, should never expect to be treated kindly. To see one negative effect of the suck-it-up philosophy, imagine that years have passed and this eight-year-old is now a teen in a relationship with an abusive boyfriend. She may stay in this abusive relationship because she does not feel she is deserving of kindness and must "suck it up". Alternatively, she could be abusive and tell everyone else to "suck it up".

In our example of the two girls, the eleven-year-old

does not feel she is being treated as an important member of the family. She is able to get away with this behavior and continues to be disrespectful. Although she knows what she is saying is negative, she learns that her negative actions do not count as negative. If her negative actions do not count, then perhaps she views herself as not counting. If she does not count, what do you think she will develop into in terms of character? Do you think she will be respectful or responsible? How could she possibly be respectful or responsible when her actions do not count? When she is not accountable? Will she hold herself accountable for her actions toward others? Will she treat herself (her body, for example) with respect?

Being respectful to oneself and others means making responsible choices about one's actions toward oneself and others.

Parents whose philosophy is to just let kids figure themselves out are quite troublesome to me. Children figure things out based on what they see and hear. Figuring it out means they are just learning from their observations and experiences. If what they are learning is just to figure it out, then they learn only through experience, not from concerned parents. Your parenting philosophy guides everything you do and the choices that you make every day. Your philosophy influences the words that you say or do not say, and the actions that you take or do not take. It is your parenting philosophy that has so much to do with who your children become.

We have become such a generation that says, "Don't blame the parents." A generation that says, "Parents should not be held responsible for their child's actions." Yes, it is true that we cannot control every choice our children make but to believe as a parent, "Don't provide guidance in the right direction for your kids because what you do and say has no impact on your child's development," is absurd.

The idea that we make our own choices separate from our upbringing is ludicrous. Everything we experience has an effect on us. Who we are arises from our experience and our upbringing, our genetics, our own inborn temperament, and our environment outside of our parents' interactions with us. If we leave out the parenting piece of the child-rearing puzzle and stop holding ourselves responsible for helping our children to learn to be respectful and responsible, then we are abandoning the extremely significant role we play in the development of our children's core values. Instead, we are simply leaving our children's growth up to whatever life brings them. This is insanity.

It is our duty as parents to help our children to develop a respectful and responsible character.

If you help your child develop a sense of respect, then he will be respectful to others and himself, and he will also ask others to respect him. Respect will be part of this child's core. He will make responsible decisions.

Respectful words and actions and making responsible choices do not exist without each other. They go hand in hand.

Chapter 2

The Dr. Karen Parenting Philosophy: Treat Your Children As Equal Members Of The Family

Take a moment to ask yourself this question: What is my parenting philosophy? If you follow the philosophy that is the focus of this chapter, your children will learn how to be respectful and responsible because that is who your child will become at his core. He will consistently interact and relate to others and to their world in a respectful and responsible manner as situations, experiences, and obstacles come his way. The Dr. Karen Parenting Philosophy, the philosophy this book is based on, is this:

Our children are truly valuable and important. Our children are equal members within the family. Therefore, they must be treated as equal members of the family.

If you expect your child to respect himself, be respectful to others, and make responsible choices, then your child needs to experience being valued. With consistency, you can help your child feel that he is just as important as everyone else in the family. This is a completely different philosophy than many of us remember hearing in our earlier days, when children were "seen but not heard." In our youth, how often did we have a choice about what Mother cooked for dinner? Many of you reading this would say,

"Never." Nowadays, children are not only considered in menu planning, but there are also all kinds of foods in the supermarket specifically created for kids. Much has changed through the years. We have learned to understand that kids do indeed have a voice in the family. As parents, therefore, we must be aware of this philosophical change, and make it work for us, for our children as individuals, and for our family as a unit.

Today's parents often feel that with the children having such a loud voice in the family, the parents themselves are no longer heard. Parents often struggle with their children over who is really in charge. Parents yell for respect just because they *are* the parents. In a generation where parents are not simply respected just because of their title in the family, they need to learn a new way to be respected. They must teach their children how to be respectful to others in and outside of the family. We now live in a world of "me, me, and only me and my needs right now." This is a world where there is neither job security nor loyalty, where people learn they need to look out for themselves because no one else will. Children often have no opportunity to learn respect and responsibility; they learn early on not to consider another's feelings because the good guy always finishes last. Children learn not to consider how their individual choices affect others.

It is our job as parents to teach our children to care about how their choices impact themselves and others, rather than only caring about their own immediate needs. This helps develop a child who makes responsible choices just because it feels right, rather than giving in to the overriding factor that we only choose what feels good for "me and only me." When you treat your child as an equal member of the family, this child learns that the choices he makes impact the whole family. The child learns that what he does matters, and has a larger effect than just on himself.

The challenge for parents who read this book is that they have to deal with other parents who do not believe in this philosophy. Your children have to deal with the other children who are not brought up with the philosophy set forth here. When you parent a child with the philosophy that he is an equal member of the family, you will often discover that the character of that child is quite different from a child who was not treated this way. Specifically, the child who is not treated as an equal member of the family often displays disrespectful and irresponsible behavior, in contrast to the child who is treated equally. This concept is explored in further detail in Chapter 12, which addresses the challenges you may face as you follow this philosophy.

Take the time to answer the following question: In order to survive and thrive in this world, do children have to demonstrate animal-like behavior? By "animal-like behavior," I mean the notion that the person with the nastiest behavior thrives. Animal-like behavior is the "eat or be eaten" philosophy. Examples include saying something mean to another, putting another down to feel better than that person, taking the toy from another rather than using verbal skills in a sharing fashion; in essence, living life as a battle, a "who is stronger than whom" way of thinking. Can the child who is respectful to others, even when others are disrespectful to him, still feel good about himself and achieve in this world? Can the child that makes responsible choices shine above those who are being irresponsible in a world where attention is usually given to the troublemaker?

There are always two sides to every coin: some children are respectful, some are not. Which side of the coin do you choose for your child? What would you like your child's character to be? Which choice leads to a child who feels happy and has a positive sense of self? Will your child grow up and become an adult who has a positive sense of self-worth?

It is this author's belief that children who develop a desire and instinct for making responsible choices will feel good about themselves. These children are the ones who will develop into happy adults with high self-esteem. If your view is in sync with mine, then read on.

Children must truly believe that they are equal members of the family. This means that they are just as important as the adults are. Children are to be seen and heard. Your children's words, opinions, thoughts, feelings, and ideas, your children's voices, are just as important as your own. You must respect them.

When I say "equal", I am not implying that you should treat your child exactly the same way you treat your spouse. This clinician is not implying that your child can decide whether the family should spend this week's salary on a video game instead of groceries. "Equal" means equally valued, just as important as, respected. It means the child's voice counts. For an example, it is disrespectful to the child to ignore his opinion to spend money on a video game. Being respectful is to address the issue. For an example, you can explain why the money should be spent on food.

When you treat your child as an equal member of the family, he then feels that you are being respectful, and the child will be respectful to you in turn. This child will also be respectful to others outside the family. Examples include but are certainly not limited to: interactions with teachers, other students at school, friends, relatives, and strangers the child encounters at museums, the ball park, the supermarket, the bank, and future work environment. You can think of other examples of places, people, and situations where you would like your children to act in a respectful manner. Consider the notion that your parenting philosophy - that is, how you interact with your child on a daily basis - *does* play a huge role in who your child is and becomes. It influences how your child relates to all those he encounters, and how he reacts to or handles life situations that come his way.

Aphorisms like: "I am the parent; therefore, do what I say," and "I am the parent, and because I am, I deserve respect," do not fly with most kids these days. How about a notion of reciprocity instead? What about the idea that respect works both ways? Children should respect their parents, and parents should respect their children. It is my philosophy that parents who act respectfully toward their children develop children who feel respected and will act respectfully toward others. Remember, "equal" means "equally valued." The child should feel like a member of the family team.

Imagine the following scenario: A boy named Frankie learns to respect his parents only because of their title as "parents." At school one day, one of the teachers says, "Frankie, please don't go down the slide head first. Please stop walking up the slide." If Frankie chooses to be respectful to the teacher just because of her title, he may obey her, but a few moments later, when the teacher turns away to deal with a different matter at the other end of the school yard, Frankie walks up the slide and goes down head first. He says to himself, "The teacher's not looking." In contrast, the child that is treated as an equal member of the family, and therefore feels respected, is a child who develops a true character at his core to behave respectfully and responsibly. So, given the same slide scenario, whether his teacher is looking or not, the child will not walk up the slide or go down headfirst again.

Often, kids do not think their parents listen to them. They say, "If my parent doesn't listen to me, then I don't have to listen to them." This statement typically comes from a kid aged between eight and eighteen. The child who feels that his voice is consistently heard in the family, even if he is not agreed with, is a child who would not even make such a comment. When I say "heard" here, I mean the child is feeling validated. The parents' ears are open and interested in what his opinions are. This is a child who is equally valued. He is an important member of the family. The child who feels listened to is typically respectful and responsible, and does indeed follow his parents' requests is likewise successful in environments outside of the house. The child who is treated as an equal member of the family is the child others (both children and adults) enjoy being around. Children very quickly pick up on the fact that this respectful child is willing and interested in working through problems, and conflict resolution conducted in a fair manner. This is the child who negotiates to resolve conflict.

In essence, other children feel respected by this child. They feel good inside when they spend time with him. The respectful child will typically veer away from a child who is out of control. The expression, "out of control" is being used here because just as adults have a hard time dealing with the disrespectful, irresponsible child, so does the child who is respectful and responsible avoid being negatively influenced and drawn in by uncontrolled behavior, but instead seeks out other respectful children. Yes, by raising your children as equal members of the family, you are actually developing a philosophy in your child that significantly impacts and helps him when he picks his social network.

The Dr. Karen Parenting Philosophy does not mean that you must do or obey everything your child says, or that the child is the boss. Rather, what is being suggested is that the child is an important part of the family team. As a fellow person in the family, the child is equally valued.

Sometimes, parents express concern that if they treat their children as equals, their children will think they can always do what they want. You are the parent. Your word is final. Kids know that. You are the boss if that is how you want to see yourself, but if you see your family as a team where *everybody* is respected and equally valued, then your child will share that philosophy. Your child will be respectful of your voice because it is your voice he values. Of course, there is a hierarchy, but within that hierarchy, it is a team. Your child knows that you are the parent. This is clear during every discussion, and the end of every discussion in which children are treated as equals is that they are able to voice their opinion, though their desires are not always granted. And who is the final decision-maker? It is the parent. The idea of treating a child as an equal member within the family means that they can express their opinions, and the rest of the family is interested in their opinions, even if they disagree. This does not mean that every discussion in this house turns into a free-for-all. On the contrary, my philosophy strongly endorses structure and rules. I discuss this in further detail in Chapter 9.

Holding the Dr. Karen Parenting Philosophy means that when your child walks out of your home, that philosophy does not just disappear. If a child is reared with the idea that he is an equal member of the family, then he feels valued and respected. The child values himself and relates respectfully to others, which in turn elicits respect from others. Once again, let me repeat that it is actually a given for your opinion, as the parent, to be the deciding factor. You do not need to force that notion down your child's throat. Of course your child's voice is not the deciding factor in a family decision. Children know that. With the Dr. Karen Parenting Philosophy, children do not get the message that they are in charge; they get the message that they are heard, valued, seen as important, and thus respected. Children need to feel that they have a voice and that their voice matters.

If you find yourself viewing your interactions with your child by saying out loud, "I am the boss, and therefore do what I say," you will not be incorporating the Dr. Karen Parenting Philosophy. If you view your parenting through the lens of the Dr. Karen Parenting Philosophy, then you should understand that you as the parent are to guide your children to learn to make responsible decisions, and to treat themselves and others respectfully. Do not, however, use that power as bossy behavior, but rather from the perspective that you are the guider or educator. If you view yourself that way, and if we are looking at the family hierarchy as a ladder, then you are actually on top of the ladder. Yes, you are then the boss, so to speak.

Under the Dr. Karen Parenting Philosophy, the family is not a true hierarchical ladder, although there is a hierarchy. More specifically, a family is a circle, each family member is a dot in that circle, and each dot affects every other dot. Sometimes, the dots stand in a line, sometimes in a triangle, sometimes in a square, and sometimes the dots go back and forth. Children affect their parents, and parents affect their children, but as the parent you are still the main educator, so yes, in charge. A client once said to me that the choices we make have a web-like effect. Indeed, the concept of a web is accurate. You are helping guide your children and influencing them just as they are influencing you; the mutual influence affects how you relate to others and how others relate to you and others.

If a child receives the impression that his parent's voice is the "final decider," then this child receives one of two impressions from his parent. One possible message the child may receive is that the parent is interested in his voice and his voice does have value and weight, that he is part of a team. Within that team, of course, if this scenario is about you the reader as the parent, then as parent, you are the one evaluating your opinion and your child's opinion, and in the end you make the final decision, though his voice counts and helps in the decision-making process. Therein lies an obvious difference in the hierarchy, as you are the one making decisions based on his voice and your own. In that you are a family team, his voice is just as important as the other voices. This first impression is a great message.

In contrast, another possible message your child may receive is that his parent is not only the final decision-maker, but *the one and only* decision-maker. This second message means that the child feels that there is no regard in the family for his voice because as a child, he has no or very little say. This message says that you are not treating your child as an equal member of the family. If you are interested in raising your child according to the Dr. Karen Parenting Philosophy, you want to give your child the first message.

A child who is consistently respected is a child who experiences that his voice counts in his home, that his opinion is valued. This is a child who feels he is an equal member of the family. It is this child who will feel responsible for his own behavior because he is important and of value in his world, which is the family unit. As his world grows, which is all other encounters outside the immediate family, he will relate in a responsible, respectful way to others. This child will take pride in making responsible choices. He will take ownership of his behaviors. He will learn that we all make choices in life, and that just because others choose to act in an irresponsible manner and display disrespectful behavior, he will not be swayed to become like them. This is the child you can trust to make wise choices.

Ask yourself now, what does the word "equal" mean to you? In the Dr. Karen Parenting Philosophy, what does equal mean, and what does equal not mean?

Picture the following scenario: A parent, named Marcie, has recently been trying to develop a routine with her five-year-old daughter, Rebecca. Specifically, after Rebecca takes off her clothes at night, she leaves them on the bathroom floor for her mother to put in the laundry basket. Marcie wants her daughter Rebecca to put her clothes in the laundry basket. This new routine has been a challenge, as Rebecca has not been following the plan. Marcie has tried using consequences with Rebecca, but that just upsets Rebecca and does not get the goal achieved. So Marcie thinks long and hard to try to figure out what technique is going to work to get Rebecca to become responsible about her belongings and her environment. Rather than using a consequence, since that technique is not working with five-year-old Rebecca (note that consequences do not always work with kids), Marcie decides to consider another philosophy. When it comes to parenting, it is this clinician's findings that successful parent-child interaction more often comes from developing the skills of responsible behavior than it does from taking things away from the child (consequences).

In an attempt to find an alternative to consequences, the parent may decide to help her daughter become more responsible by creating a game out of the responsibility. For an example, Marcie can time her daughter on how fast Rebecca can undress and put her clothes in the laundry basket. Then Marcie can explain that she can time Rebecca again the next day and see if she can beat her record. Perhaps as Rebecca becomes used to this idea, it becomes her routine. Once putting her clothes in the laundry basket becomes her routine, Marcie notices that Rebecca develops a routine on her own by counting out loud. It is important that the parent provide her child with positive feedback for being so fast and beating her record from the day before. Marcie can also tell Rebecca how exciting Rebecca's great counting skills are.

Or, as another tactic, perhaps the parent needs to change out of her work clothes at the same time, and so the parent decides to race the daughter. Both the parent and child get undressed and put their own clothes in the laundry baskets in their respective rooms. Then, parent and child meet in the hall once their change of clothes are on.

In the example of Marcie and her five-year-old daughter Rebecca, the mother created an experience of acting responsibly as fun. Thus, the child has the opportunity to develop a feeling of fun attached to acting responsibly. When a child associates fun with being responsible, she develops a good feeling.

Now picture another example: Your sixteen-year-old son, Jimmy does not put his laundry in the basket. Jimmy's consequence is that you give him only half of his allowance. (This consequence was already agreed on.) He continues to leave his dirty basketball clothes on the floor of the main bathroom and his clothes from school on the couch in the family room. Soon, Jimmy protests that he feels it is unfair that he gets penalized for his actions, whereas his younger sister does not. In first considering the Dr. Karen Parenting Philosophy, you may wonder how it is possible to treat everyone equally if everyone is different in the family. Each family member is different; e.g., differences in age, gender, personality, and needs.

The Dr. Karen Parenting Philosophy is not about treating everyone as equals with the implication that you would respond to problems with the same solution. Treating your children as equal members within the family is about treating each child with equal respect and value, as you would yourself and your spouse. It is about considering each person as an individual, and being kind to each person on that person's level. It is about respecting the personality and needs of each individual person.

Therefore, if you are respecting everyone equally and valuing them equally, that means that you would absolutely consider their needs, developmental stage, personality, and so forth in all of the decisions you make. Therefore, in the example of the sixteen- year-old boy, the parent should discuss with him why he is getting the consequences approach. Furthermore, do discuss his opinion and his feelings about the approach you are using for his younger sister. Allow him a voice to express how he feels the problem should be handled in his opinion. Of course, as the parent you will be the final decision-maker. For the parent of a teenager, interest in his opinion is imperative if you are going to apply the Dr. Karen Parenting Philosophy.

It is in the nine key techniques where you will learn nine specific, concrete ways to incorporate this parenting philosophy successfully. Are you ready for the next part of your journey? Now that you have read about the Dr. Karen Parenting Philosophy, the next step is as follows:

Imagine this parenting philosophy as the key to unlocking the door to raising respectful and responsible children. Next, imagine nine grooves on the key. Each groove is a technique; each one is needed to make up this very special key to fit in the door.

Your parenting philosophy guides your thoughts and actions. It is the lens through which one views parenting, and influences the actions we take as parents. The techniques parents use help to move a theory, a philosophy into action.

CHAPTER 3

TECHNIQUE #1: HEAR THE VOICE OF YOUR CHILD

The technique of hearing the voice of your child drives the overall parenting philosophy presented in this book. It is this technique intertwined within each of the other techniques that take the Dr. Karen Parenting Philosophy from a theory into a reality of action form.

No matter how seemingly absurd whatever your child is saying or asking of you is, no matter what the point that your child is trying to make is, no matter what your child's age is, if you are going to implement Technique #1, "Hear the Voice of Your Child," then you must not brush him off. What do I mean by brushing off? Ignoring, not responding, responding with an attitude that your child's statement or question is not worthy of your time, stating that you do not have time to consider your child's question or opinion, or considering his ideas to be nonsense.

Hearing the voice of your child means that your child's opinion does count.

No matter how tired you are at the end of the day, *do not ignore your child's voice.* It is human to be tired or just not in the mood to address, respond to, discuss, and/or explore what your child just said. Maybe you think it is absurd. Perhaps your child has certain emotional challenges, psychological disabilities, or perhaps he is just simply saying something that you feel does not warrant a response. But remember this: what your child is verbalizing is not absurd to him. Perhaps you feel that a reply would just be humoring your child and you do not have the time to do that. I am here to tell you that if your sincere desire is to raise a child who is respectful and makes responsible choices, then you are making a grave error in judgment if you act in a dismissive manner toward your child, even if you are tired or not in the mood.

We are all busy. Is that not sad, what our lives have come to? We choose to have children and are blessed to have them when others are struggling to conceive. It is kind and respectful to tell your child that you are feeling tired right now and to apologize for not having the full energy to respond to what he is saying right now. "Right now" is the key phrase. It means you will respond later. Tell your child that you are hoping it will be okay with him if you take a rain check on the discussion. Say clearly that you are looking forward to hearing more of the details of what he wants to share with you, but you want to do this at another time. Be as specific as you can when "another time" is. If you need a good night's rest, then say that tomorrow morning will be a good time and you are looking forward to speaking with him. If you need time to cook dinner and put on your pajamas, and then you will be ready to explore his questions, tell him that. This technique will take you far in helping your child learn to show respect for others and himself, and to make responsible choices in general. It is better to communicate to your child that you want to hear his voice a little later than to say nothing and express through your body language that what your child wants to say is just not worthy of your time.

It is not okay for your child to receive the message from you that his voice does not count. If you want your child to be respectful and make responsible choices, if you want your child to feel good about himself, then it is imperative that you hear his voice. Otherwise, there is a much higher likelihood that he will hear neither your voice nor the voices of others.

Keep in mind that you must make sure to follow through. If you say to your child, "Tomorrow morning, I would like to hear what it is you are trying to tell me right now," then make sure that you keep that date. If you say, "I just need a few minutes to wash my face and go to the bathroom, then I want to hear what you have to say," make sure that you follow up. If you cannot specify when you know you will have the patience to attend to your child, then do not give a specific day and time. Instead, say, "Can I let you know when a more comfortable time for me to pay you the attention that you deserve and hear what you are trying to say to me would be?" When you are ready to talk to your child, whether this is within a few hours or the following day, be sure to follow up. Do not go past the next day.

It is important to hear your child's voice, even if you do not agree with him. Do not discount or disrespect your child. Treat him like an equal member of the family. When you do not hear your child's voice, this makes him feel devalued, as if his words are not worthy of your attention. Putting your child's statements and questions off, whether by a few minutes, or hours, must not become the pattern. You want your child to feel that you are interested in interacting with him when he is interested in interacting with you. This helps to develop a child with positive self-worth.

Remember that you want to be respectful to your child. If, more often than not, your child is getting the message that you are putting him off, that is what he will learn. You will see that he puts off his responsibilities.

For example, suppose that every time you say, "Please take out the garbage," your fourteen-year-old son says, "Later." Later comes, but the garbage has not been taken out. His timeline for doing his chores may be different from yours. If he communicates his needs to you, as you communicate your needs to him, and both of you say clearly and respectfully when the task needs to be done, a wonderful, positive snowball effect occurs. When your son says, "Mom, I really need you to drive me to Zach's house by 9 a.m. on Sunday," you will be able to make it happen for him. It works the same way when you then say to your son, "I really need you to take out the garbage before 7 a.m. on Thursday." There will, however, be times you cannot follow through for him just as he may not be able to follow through for you. The key is to be respectful about not being able to do what the other is asking. The goal is not to turn your every interaction into a conflict-ridden, full-out brawl. The goal is for you both to be respectful. The cycle of interaction is hearing each other's voices.

Here are some age-related examples of applying Technique #1.

INFANTS

If your infant is crying during the night, you can choose to go into his bedroom and attempt to comfort the child. You can also let your child cry. The philosophy of treating your infant as an equal member of the family suggests that you go into your child's room and try to understand what is leading to the crying behavior, then trying to help. Think about this for a moment. If your spouse says he is feeling very lonely today and a hug would really help, would you not respond to him? Would you walk away? Would you ignore him? (If your answer is yes, then perhaps my next book on helping your marriage might be in order!)

If you do not go to your infant when he is crying, this is exactly what you are doing from the infant's point of view: ignoring him. If you are not responding to your infant or your spouse, not going in to comfort him, that is disrespectful. If you would respond to your infant or spouse with affection when he requests it, then you are respectful to him. Bear in mind that "equal" does not always mean "exactly the same at the same moment at the same time." Equal does mean treating each member as important and valued. From the infant's point of view, you are ignoring his voice if you do not go in to his room. Your infant is expressing his feelings in the only way an infant can: through crying. If you consistently do not attend to your infant's crying, what he learns is this: "I am not a valued member of this family, and no one will help me if I need help." This infant further says to himself, "I am not respected. Perhaps then, I am not worthy of respect, if even the people who are supposed to love me are not listening to my voice."

Consider how this experience in infancy carries into the child's personality as he ages. Imagine, for an example, your preschool child cuts in front of another child in line at school, and the other child says, "Hey, that's not fair! You hurt my feelings." Your preschooler shrugs his shoulders as if to say, "Too bad." Your child learned in infancy that if he cries, it is too bad. No one comes to help him. As a preschooler, that is how he responds and treats others. In essence, if your child learns his voice is not valued, then he does not learn the value of considering another's voice. If your child does learn that his voice is valued, then he will instinctively be respectful of others because of his consistent experiences.

Consider another example. Time has passed, this same infant is older, and he is in elementary school. After class one day, this child and another child are standing with their teacher discussing an assignment, and the teacher drops the book she is holding and it almost hits the child's foot. This child looks down and waits for the teacher to pick the book up. Or perhaps he is annoyed and looks down at the book and pushes it with his toe. The child who learned as an infant that another comes to his aid will be the child who picks up the book as a respectful gesture. In contrast, the child who learned to fend for himself in infancy may be lacking in respect and courtesy, and thus does not help the teacher.

If you were sad, would you expect and hope that someone in your family would hear your voice and ask you what was bothering you? Would you assume that a family member may ask you if there was something they could do to help you feel better? Actually, one should expect that.

That expectation is an appropriate expectation. It is a shame that too many people do not have that expectation met. That unmet expectation causes much pain and significantly impacts who that child becomes as an adult. The same responsive behavior applies to your infant. If your infant is expressing a need that is not met, it instills in that infant a sense of not being valued, of not being important enough for his parents to stop what they are doing and come to his aid. He has learned that his parents do not hear his voice.

Treating your infant as an equal member of the family requires that you respond to his crying by coming into his room and saying that you heard his crying. If it is your parenting philosophy that your infant needs to learn to "self-soothe," then you should at least have the decency to communicate this philosophy to your infant. For an example, walk into his room and tell him your agenda. However, communicating to your infant your parenting plan would be giving your infant the respectful interaction of the Dr. Karen Parenting Philosophy. This may be seen as odd to those that do not value an infant's voice and do not consider the infant's voice as an equal member of the family.

Your actions today do indeed affect your child's development. As a parent, you have an impact. To think otherwise is ignorance. Much has been written over the years about who is to blame when it comes to a child's actions. Is the blame to be placed on genetics or the environment? But this book is not about blame; it is about recognizing the importance of each adult parent as an individual taking ownership for one's actions, and treating each person in one's family as a person of value. This book is about recognizing that parents play a role in teaching their children to behave respectfully and make responsible choices. There are things parents can do today to make a difference.

PRESCHOOLERS

Before parents truly understand what "hearing your child's voice" really means, they often express concern and surprise at the concept. I have heard parents say, "Who is in charge? Me or my kid?" This implies that when you hear your child's voice, it somehow means you are doing everything your child wants all of the time, and you have no power. This is not the case. You have more power (if you want to call it that) over another person's actions if that person feels you are interested in his voice. Hearing your child's voice means treating his opinions as important and being respectful of his thoughts, feelings, comments, opinions, and questions. I have heard parents say, "I don't want my child to learn that everything he says is up for discussion. I am the parent. What I say, goes." That parent may be thinking she does not want to take the time to discuss with her child why she has made certain choices. But you do not have to explain everything. Some things are just for grown-up ears. But certainly there are many things kids can and should hear. Take the time out to explain to them what your thinking is *and* give them the respect to hear theirs.

One of the errors a parent can make to decrease the chances that their child will learn to be respectful and make responsible choices is to not allow them to have a voice. As already discussed, if you recognize that your child does have a voice, and your philosophy is that his voice counts and your child is an equal member of the family, then you will be helping your child become a person who is respectful and makes responsible choices.

Picture the following scenario: Your three-year-old asks, "Can we go out to eat at the restaurant that has the video games to play? Can we go RIGHT NOW?" Imagine the direct way in which this child asked this question. Hear the assertiveness in his tone. Take a moment to visualize this situation. You are exhausted. You have been out all day. Perhaps you have spent the day with your child doing fun things with him, or perhaps you were at work all day outside the home. Either way, you are tired. Now imagine that you have just finished cooking dinner. At this point, you can barely stand up. Your back is killing you from the strain of standing and cooking for so long, combined with the stress and tension of something that happened that day that is creating muscle tension. What you may be thinking is, "You've got to be kidding me! Yeah, right. Like that's what we are going to do right now. I am so freakin' exhausted, and I just cooked dinner. Does anyone appreciate what I am doing here? Didn't I do enough today already?" Typically in this situation, parents would just say no, or no along with a further statement like, "Go out and play," or, "Your father is almost home." Or you may just ignore your child's request and not respond. Or you may just simply say, "Go wash your hands for dinner." Perhaps you may get mean and say, "Are you crazy? No way. I just cooked dinner. Give me a break." Although all of these responses might not seem negative from a parent's point of view, to a three-year-old, they are downright disrespectful. Certainly, the child does not feel that his voice was heard.

Imagine on a different day, this same three-year-old just had a pee and poop accident and you asked him to put his wet underwear in the garbage. If he said, "No way. I just put my pants in the laundry bag. Give me a break," you would think he was being disrespectful, right? Well, the same is true for how the child might feel about your response to his restaurant question. Any of the parental responses given above has the potential to grow into a full-fledged power struggle, a full argument with a freak-out by your three-year-old.

In a power struggle, your child may speak louder and keep asking the same questions over and over again to try to get you to hear him and get his way. An argument is what a power struggle is. Imagine the freak-out of your child on the floor with tears rolling down his face, yelling so loud that your ears start to ring as you hear him crying, "You never do what I want. I want to go out to eat to the restaurant with the video games!" The freak-out occurs as a power struggle because the child did not feel that his opinion was heard. It is not just about him wanting to go to wherever it is he wants to go anymore; it turns into him not feeling that his voice was respected, that his voice was not heard, not important or valued. In essence, he did not feel he was an equal member of the family. Next, he became belligerent and disrespectful. What your child is actually doing is fighting for his voice, and this fighting often leads to poor and irresponsible choices.

It is human nature to defend ourselves. When a child feels unheard and devalued, his typical instinct is to try to get heard in self-defense of one's position. For an example, now that he is freaking out, he grabs his baseball and hurls it across the room. The ball hits your favorite picture. The glass breaks all over the floor. His throwing the ball in the house is irresponsible behavior that could have been prevented. This is a clear example of escalation that could have absolutely been prevented if the Dr. Karen Parenting Philosophy and Technique #1, Hear Your Child's Voice had been used.

If you and your child argue consistently over time because he does not feel his voice is heard, and he consistently reacts disrespectfully and irresponsibly, this becomes the pattern. Instead, if this child is given opportunities to develop into a person who is respectful and makes responsible choices, that will become the pattern. He will see himself as respectful and responsible, and that is who he will become. Hearing your child's voice is imperative. It will give your child successful opportunities to be respectful and make positive choices.

It is important to know that hearing your child's voice does not always mean doing what your child is requesting. Hearing your child's voice does not necessarily mean obeying him. *Hearing your child's voice specifically means that you must validate his point of view.* In the example of the three-year-old wanting to go to a restaurant with video games, you might say something along the lines of, "Oh, that would be so much fun. We always have so much fun when we go there. I am so sorry, honey, really, I am sorry we cannot go there tonight. We absolutely have to plan a day and a time to go there again because I know you have a great time there. Come here, honey. Let me give you a juicy hug. Let's plan that, okay? Do you definitely want to plan a day to go there?" Now you have heard your child's voice. You have validated what he said, so there is nothing to fight about. There is no argument, no freak-out on the floor, no anger. You validated your child's feelings when you heard his voice by responding respectfully.

Hearing your child's voice is responding in a way that is respectful of his opinion, showing him that his opinion counts, and showing that you sincerely understand his point of view by restating it. In this example, you mirrored your child's statement by saying, "It would be so much fun," and "We will plan a time." The child is thinking it would be fun to go to the restaurant. He is thinking that he would like to plan a time for this. When you validate his feelings, you are using Technique #1. You have heard his voice. This also helps him to learn the skill of expressing his feelings with words instead of freaking out. Instead of having a freak-out right back at him or ignoring his words, you said what he was thinking. Hearing your child's voice is a technique for getting to know your child.

When you use Technique #1 with your preschooler and hear his voice, you have removed the power struggle around who is going to win. By saying the restaurant is fun, you took the time to validate his point of view, and you treated him with respect as an equal member of the family by explaining in a rational way why today is not the day to go. You did not dismiss his idea as invalid and imply that his opinion does not count. Telling him that going out to a restaurant is not going to happen today lets him hear your voice. Since you spoke in a respectful manner, he felt that his voice was just as valued as yours.

The next step is to make sure that you give your child positive feedback for understanding your opinion. Tell him you appreciate it that he handled not getting to do what he wanted right now in such a respectful and responsible manner. Giving your child positive feedback reinforces his positive behavior, so he acts like that again the next time a similar situation arises where he does not get his way. Positive feedback also helps him see himself as respectful and responsible.

Temper tantrums can often be prevented by consistently using Technique #1. If, time and time again, your child is listened to, you will find that he does not resort to acting disrespectfully. By using Technique #1 you are helping your child become a respectful and responsible person in your view of him, and thus in his view of himself.

It is the consistency of events throughout a child's childhood that helps them develop into who they see themselves as, and how they relate to the world around them, thereby affecting how others relate to them, and their ongoing development of how they see themselves.

Sometimes, listening to your child's voice means specifically validating and respecting without obeying the child's wishes, whereas other times, it means actually obeying your child. The following story is about having true respect for your child's voice, and considering it in your decision-making process; not only respecting it with words, but also obeying it out of respect for your child, even if another adult may see this as strange. There will always be some who frown at the Dr. Karen Parenting Philosophy. Here is a story that is an example of a parent listening to her child's voice but was frowned upon by another parent. It is a personal example taken from the memoirs of this clinician. I will discuss the notion of others disagreeing with the Dr. Karen Parenting Philosophy in Chapter 12.

My son had just turned five. There was a girl in his class who was interested in having a play date with him. In fact, when I took him to school, I could never walk by her without her asking, "When can I have a play date with Jeremy?" What this child did not know was that when she was four years old, her mother had told me that because my philosophy of child rearing was so different from hers, our children could not be friends outside of school.

When the children were four, they had had several play dates at my house. The girl's mother would always drop her off at the start of the play date and pick her up when it was over. The mother had a lovely block of time to get her errands done. The girl always told her mother how much fun she had. Many children of four years of age are not ready for a play date without their parent remaining, whereas others are. Some parents of four-year-old children may not be ready for a drop-off play-date for the first time at a friend's house, but then after a few times they feel comfortable.

When the mother came to pick up her daughter, I always made it a point to share with her what some of the activities were that the kids did. My parenting style is one of interest in what my son and his friends are doing, as well as whether he and the other child are happy. It is important to be aware of what is occurring with one's children, and a parent of a four-year-old should absolutely have her eyes and ears open to what is occurring in their home. I soon found out this mother preferred not to know, and her parenting resembled this philosophy.

Eventually, the mother asked about having my son over to her house. I replied that he enjoyed playing with her daughter very much and would love to come over, but that I would need to come with him, at least for the first play date, and possibly for the first few. I explained that my son had said very clearly that he was not ready yet to have a play date at a house he had never been to without my being there first. Now, I consider that very reasonable. My son wanted to make sure it was safe. He was being a smart boy. He wanted to have time to evaluate this situation to develop his own opinion, with me there to give him a sense of safety and security. The other mother looked at me oddly, as though she thought me listening to my son's voice was ridiculous, as though I should set the rules for when it was time for him to have a play date without me being there. My philosophy is that if we hear our children's voice, they will develop their own good judgment in themselves.

My son learned that I had confidence in his inner voice, and therefore he learned to have confidence in it, too. If his inner voice told him that he wanted me to come along, and I listened, then that inferred that I trusted his inner voice. He would feel confident that, with me there, he could evaluate the situation and determine on his own if he felt it was safe to go back next time without me. This is how a child learns that he has a trustworthy inner voice.

After that conversation, the other mother told me that because I "hover," my son could not visit her house. Yes, she felt that my hearing his voice about attending his first play date at her house would be hovering. She explained that she did not want her daughter seeing that a mother would stay at a play date. Oh, my! Might her daughter see another child's mother respecting a child's voice? Might her child ask her mother to respect her voice? Would that be a situation of concern for this mother? Yes, "hover" is the word parents sometimes use when they are uninterested in their children's world, and would rather focus on their own selfish world. This does not mean that there is no such thing as a hovering parent; there certainly are parents that hover. But in this story, we see a fine example of the difference between a parent who hears her child's voice and one who does not; it is not a hovering parent, rather a parent that follows the Dr. Karen Parenting Philosophy.

The other mother said, "Unless Jeremy can come without you, then he cannot come over." That is when she further explained that due to the difference in our parenting philosophies, our children could not be friends outside of school. My knowing what was going on in my home when the children were playing together, having my eyes and ears open enough to let her know what the kids did together, and listening to my son's voice, was too overwhelming for her free style of parenting. On a personal note, of course I am glad that I listened to my son's voice. It became abundantly clear that if my son was at her house, and he were injured or just simply needed help with something, she would not know it because her ears and eyes were not open to what was going on. If she did not care about the events taking place with her own child, how could I expect her to care for my child? I actually felt sad for her daughter, as I foresaw many problems to come based on this type of decision-making by the mother.

When it comes to young kids, you can indeed have your ears and eyes open to what is going on in your home without hovering. You can give the children their time together, their space and privacy, but all the while you are within earshot. A parent can help one's young child to feel she is playing independently along with the feeling that if help is needed, the parent is close by and available. Their young minds are developing. As a parent, you should want your child to be at a play date where you know the other parent's ears and eyes are open to know what the kids are up to. Do not put your head in the sand. When you look up, you may not like what you see.

It is very important to listen carefully to what your children are saying because they often have a very important opinion, perhaps a sense of something before you do. Not everyone will agree with the Dr. Karen Parenting Philosophy; some may even find it offensive. Yes, there will be times when other parents may respond negatively to your parenting stance. They may question your choices. Dr. Karen is here to say that you should be prepared for that.

Stand up for what you believe in by raising your children by the Dr. Karen Parenting Philosophy if this is what you want to do. What others do is their choice; you cannot control them. I neither tried to defend my position nor tried to change the other mother's stance. I wished her the best. To my readers, I suggest you do not feel obligated to educate others if they have their own parenting philosophy.

The plan is to focus on doing your best to raise your children. I hope that sharing my personal experience of facing a parent who disagreed with my philosophy helps you on your voyage of raising your children.

ELEMENTARY AND MIDDLE SCHOOLERS

Elementary and middle school children face a lot of challenging situations. They have heavy emotions and are trying to understand their thoughts. They need compassion. This is the age when parents slowly lose their emotional connection with their kids, sometimes without even realizing it. Kids in this age range are much more independent than when they were younger. At times, they seem to be mini-adults. As you continue to help them achieve independence, it is important to still be there for them. They need to know you are there for them emotionally.

Picture the following scenario of a nine-year-old experiencing separation anxiety each time she departs from her mother. She is so anxious that she vomits as the separation is about to occur. Then she smears the vomit all over her walls in her room. In this example, the mother sees this child as being disrespectful and making very poor choices by smearing the vomit and making a mess in her room. The parent who is not hearing the child's voice will be the parent whose child continues to display the anxiety symptoms (vomiting, smearing). An example of the parent that does not hear the voice of one's child: She may often assume that if she makes light of the problem by saying, "There is nothing to worry about," then the problem will stop. Another example of a parent not hearing the voice of one's child: She may become frustrated and react with anger and say, "Clean up your room this instant! This is no way to get my attention. You are going to have to just deal with me leaving and just suck it up." Another example is the parent who says, "If you do this again, I am going to smear your face in your throw-up." Clearly these parents are not hearing the child's voice. This disrespectful response to one's child certainly increases the chances of raising a child who will most likely not be respectful or make responsible choices. This is the child who is not seeing respect or responsible choices from her parent. This is also the child who does not experience the feeling of supportive understanding. Therefore, the child typically will not provide supportive understanding to others.

To hear your child's voice, you must enter into your child's mind, so to speak. Be patient. Take time from your busy day to ask yourself what your child is experiencing. Do not hesitate to ask your child. Sometimes, parents are afraid to ask their child what she is thinking because they are afraid they may put thoughts that do not already exist into their child's head, or may somehow make it worse by talking about it. Have confidence in your own ability to communicate. Have confidence in your child that she can explain what she is feeling. Maybe she can even tell you what she thinks she needs in order to feel better. *Often, children have the answers to their own problems, and they just need you to guide that solution so that it works.* What you need to do to develop the right solution is hear your child's voice. It is when you are not hearing your child's voice that no solution can work because it is not a good fit.

The following is a step-by-step process you can follow in many situations when you are interested in applying Technique #1. This process is not just for elementary and middle school children. You can also use it with younger and older children. Let your child's age and personality guide your conversational style, as you apply the steps appropriate to your situation. As you read the following steps, consider a situation you are currently experiencing with your child, and/or have experienced. I will use the example of the nine-year-old girl as I take you through the steps.

Step #1. *Sit down with your child when there are no distractions. Give your child your full attention, with the goal of discussing the situation with her and trying to hear her voice.*

Step #2. *Focus on normalizing your child's behavior so she does not feel so bad about herself, and experience self-hatred.*

The odds are she is already feeling bad about the pattern of behavior. Say to her, "Honey, I have noticed that each time we leave each other, you vomit. I think I have an idea about why that is happening. Can I share with you why I think you are vomiting? If I understand this correctly, will you tell me so? If I don't understand and I am wrong, would you tell me that?" After your child responds, you can say something along these lines: "I think you are vomiting as a reaction to being nervous or afraid or concerned or worried about something when we are apart from one another. It is normal to feel discomfort when apart from a parent. I think many kids have that experience. Maybe if we talked about your worry, I could help you feel better.

Maybe you smear it on the wall in your room because you are feeling bad about the situation and don't know what else to do."

Wait for your child's response. You can then say something like, "You know, I heard that some people cry when they get nervous, not just kids, but adults, too. Some people get belly aches, some people get back aches, some people get headaches, and some people get eye twitches." Explain to your child that some people's bodies react to their feelings. At this point, depending on her age and personality, your child may ask you some questions. Take your time and discuss the concept that when a person is concerned about something, some people respond in one way, but would prefer to respond differently. Discuss the problem as a resolvable challenge. Once someone understands why she is behaving the way she is, there are other choices.

You can say, "Together, we can figure out a way for you to not feel so nervous. I can't imagine that it feels good to feel nervous. And it must feel awful to vomit. Do you think it is possible that you are feeling nervous about my leaving and that is why your body then throws up? Or do you think it is something else that is causing the vomit?" This gives your child the opportunity to think about this and try to understand how she is feeling. She also knows that you are trying to hear her voice. You are trying to understand what the vomit and her actions are saying. The parent who is worried that by giving attention to that awful behavior will be giving the child what she wants is the parent who is not hearing her child's voice. Sometimes, parents are concerned that their child is manipulating them.

But children want to be heard. As the parent, it is your job to listen and not feel manipulated.

Step #3. *Make sure you hear her voice and that she feels you understand what she is saying.*

The key to successfully implementing Step #3 is to ask questions that make sure you understand why she is feeling those emotions, and what vision she foresees that she is afraid will happen. Tell your child that you would like to understand why she is vomiting. Explain further that you have questions to ask her so that she can try to help you to understand how she is feeling. Tell her you really care about her feelings and want to help her. You can use questions like these: "Are you afraid something is going to happen to you?" "Are you afraid something is going to happen to me?" "Are you not sure what you are afraid of, but you are feeling generally afraid?" "If you are not feeling afraid, is it something else? Are you feeling nervous, sad, or angry?"

Ask your child, "What word can we put to what you are feeling when I am going to leave? Can you tell me?" Do not be afraid to ask questions. "Has something bad ever happened to you when we were apart from each other? Is this what you are thinking about when I am away from you? Is this something you never told me? Did you hear about something that happened to another kid when they were away from their parents, and you are concerned that will happen to you?" With each question, wait patiently for a response. If your child does not respond, still remain patient and ask your child if these things are hard to talk about. You do not want your child to feel pressured to answer. You want her to feel that you are interested in hearing her voice. Then she will want to answer your questions. If your child feels you are genuinely interested, she will want to speak openly. She will understand that you want to work toward a resolution, and you are not judging her.

Step #4. *Once you have gotten an understanding of what your child is feeling, make sure to validate her voice.*

Validation means repeating her feelings back to her to make sure you are clear on what she is saying. Then you will be able to develop a solution that fits the problem. Validation will allow your daughter to feel that her voice is truly being heard, even before you begin to search for a solution. For some children, just knowing they are being heard is all they need for a behavioral change. For example, your child answers, "I get nervous when you leave because I am afraid that something bad might happen to you." You can validate it by saying something like, "Oh, honey, that must be so scary for you. It must be so hard for you that when I leave you are scared that something bad might happen to me." You can further validate her feelings by saying, "What a scary thing for a child to feel about their parents that they love so much." Validation is not necessarily agreement that you think her fear is going to come true, or that you are also afraid something bad might happen. Validation is clearly letting your child know that you are truly hearing what she is saying.

Step #5. *If going up to Step #4 is all your child needs for certain situations, then that is great and will suffice. If there needs to be a fifth step that goes beyond validation and into developing an actual solution, then that is what Step #5 is: developing a solution with your child that fits.*

Sometimes, the solution is a simple reassurance. Other times, the solution is much more complicated. Whatever the situation is, here is how to develop a solution. First, say, "Let's work together as a team to figure out what we can come up with to solve the problem." Specify what the actual problem is *and* what the symptoms are. The next step is to ask questions and pay close attention to your child's answers. Discuss her answers and be sure to incorporate the steps given above to hear your child's voice. You want to be sure you are hearing your child's ideas for a solution. Key questions you should ask include:

1. Is there anything I can do or say to help _____?

2. Is there anything you can do or say to help _____?

3. Is there anything that if that happened it would help _____?

Parents, where you see the _____, that is where you want to state what the problem is and what the symptoms are.

In this example, you may consider saying something like, "Honey, is there anything that I can do or say to help you to not feel so scared that something bad is going to happen to me? Is there something I can do or say so you won't feel worried about being away from me so you vomit and then choose to smear it on the wall?" Wait for your child's response. Notice how you say "so you vomit" and "*choose* to smear it on the wall." It is important to consider your words and use them wisely.

As you develop a solution, you can explain to your child

that now that she knows that you understand why she is vomiting, she does not have to *choose* to smear it. You can work as a team on her not feeling so uncomfortable and worried (the problem), so that she does not vomit (the symptom of the problem), and then smear it (her chosen reaction). You will often find that your child's solution is quite helpful in generating an actual solution. Sometimes, children have an idea that is quite feasible if you work with them to find the solution that uses both their idea and yours. Sometimes, children already have within them what they need to help them. The key to helping your child generate a solution that fits is to listen to her ideas. Listen patiently to your child's voice.

For example, if your child says, "If you call me on the telephone every ten minutes when I am with the babysitter to let me know that you are safe, that might work." To validate her, you can say, "Calling you. What a great idea." Confirm her opinion and further validate it and reinforce its greatness. You might say something like, "So you think if I call you often, like every ten minutes, you won't be so afraid that something bad might happen to me? If you aren't feeling nervous about that, then maybe the vomit won't come out?" You may also provide a positive prediction of the future. For example, you can say, "In fact, you might even be able to enjoy doing one of your favorite activities with your sitter instead of missing out on that fun time."

Now you have heard her voice telling you what the problem is, and how she thinks it can be solved. She now feels heard. To make it work, explore options with her. Ask her if she thinks if maybe the next time the sitter comes, you have to call her every ten minutes, or if she thinks she might handle every twenty minutes. Then ask her if every thirty minutes, or once an hour, would be doable. Ask her to help you with a plan for the third, fourth, and fifth babysitting experiences. Let her know that you will ask her how this solution is working and how she is feeling. Tell her you want to know that the solutions you developed as a team is working the way that is desired and hoped for.

In developing a solution that fits, you should incorporate what you have learned from the previous steps. In this example, if her vision is a car accident, you can discuss what safety precautions you are taking: you are wearing a seat belt and keeping your eyes on the road. If her concern is different, the point is that by knowing what it is, you can help her. If she does not propose a solution (telephone calls), say, "Would you like us to put our heads together to figure out an idea of what would help?" Express your confidence that if you work together as a team, you will figure out how to help her not feel so scared.

Exploring your child's ideas helps her to feel better when she divulges her concern. It is when a child's voice is stifled that the child's feelings come out in negative ways that parents view as disrespectful or irresponsible.

TEENAGERS

Parents of disrespectful teens who do not make responsible choices are often looking for ideas that will help them redirect problematic behavior. One of the most common complaints that is an obstacle, I hear from parents of teens is as follows: Parents of teenagers have a long history with their children, thus they may not be willing to hear their teenager's voice if they feel their teen has not been hearing their voice for years.

There are different types of cases with teens. In some cases, there has been a decline in the parent-child relationship for years, with parents believing that the shift began during the elementary and school years. Other parents look back on their child's preschool years and say their child has always been disrespectful, and always made irresponsible choices. Other parents report that the moment their child became a teenager it was like a light switch flipped, and the kid's personality changed. Whatever your case may be, it is imperative that teenagers also experience their parent as hearing their voice.

Parents often report that they feel their child should hear the parental voice, not the other way around. Some parents have reported not only frustration but even bitter resentment and feelings of betrayal when it comes to their teenager's lack of respect. This makes it even more challenging to consider making a parental shift in how they interact with their teenager. Parents and teenagers need to hear each other's voices. Listening has to work in both directions. It is never too late to make a shift in your parenting philosophy. Although it takes two to tango, you may need to take the lead and start a new dance. It takes only one member of a parent-child relationship to begin the process of making a positive shift.

I have also found that some parents consider using Technique #1 before they completely understand it, and sometimes even after they think they understand it. They report concern that their teenager will take advantage of them if they suddenly become "nice." I find it intriguing that this technique is often seen as being nice. Parents report the concern that if they hear their teen's voice and are therefore seen as nice, that would be perceived as "giving him his way." I have heard parents express concern that their teen will manipulate them if they see any sign of weakness. Yes, some parents wonder if hearing their teen's voice can make them seem weak.

Once parents fully grasp this technique by trying it and seeing positive results, they begin to recognize that being respectful can elicit respectful behavior back to them. You will not be perceived as weak, nor are you "giving him his way" in a power struggle in which your teenager wins and gets his way and you lose. There is not a winner and loser with Technique #1, only winners. Let us take the power struggle out of the mix by giving your teenager the respect you want from him. Your teen is an equal member of your family; give him the respect you feel you deserve.

The parent-child relationship is filled with moments when a power struggle can occur. You can end power struggles in your relationship with your teenager by hearing his voice. You are being respectful of your teenager and interested in his view, taking his view as significant, valuing his opinion, and treating it as something of worth. Parents often express their confusion about how to incorporate Technique #1 into parenting. If you do not hear your teen's voice, your teen, more than likely, will not hear your voice or the voices of others. If you hear your teen's voice, he will more than likely hear your voice and the voices of others. Your teen will be respectful to you and your needs, as well as the needs of others, like his friends and teachers. Your teenager will make positive, responsible choices.

The questions a parent of a teen asks include the following: "How do I apply this technique with my teen?" "How does that lead to my teen being respectful and making responsible choices?" Imagine the following scenario. Your fourteen-year-old announces, "I'm going out tonight." The recent pattern has been that your teen does not tell you where he is going. In fact, when you ask, he either lies or gets annoyed at you for even asking and says something to you in a nasty tone. Perhaps he is so disrespectful that he even slams the door in your face. Perhaps he curses at you. Since you feel he is being disrespectful to you, you enter the same behavior zone by arguing with him, after which there is an escalation that does not result in a positive outcome. It is a lose-lose situation. It is a power struggle. In this case, also imagine that this teen has not been obeying the curfew you set for him.

Win-win in this scenario means that your teen tells you where he is going in a respectful manner and comes home on time without arguments. No more nasty behavior, no more cursing, no more disrespect. When you feel respected and he does not experience a power struggle, he also feels respected, so you both win.

Teenagers often report that they feel their parents are torturing them with interrogations about where they are going. Teens report that being asked where they are going makes them feel like their parent does not trust them. They also report that they feel suffocated. They report that they feel like the only way to get their parent to "stop bugging them" is to act rude because sometimes the parent will just walk away in frustration, and finally the teen has some peace and quiet. Teenagers also claim that their parents are treating them like a baby. These feelings arise when it comes to questions of where they are going, who they are going out with, and when they are coming home.

When it comes right down to it, you love your child. You are concerned about his welfare. You want him to be safe. But your teen is not hearing that side of your thoughts. What your teen is hearing is a lack of trust, an interrogation, and a power-struggle. He feels trapped and unable to be independent. He is not hearing love and care in your voice. To regain control, not of you but of himself, he pushes back. It is not that he is trying to get under your skin by not listening to your rules. Your teen wants to feel in control of himself. If he does not feel he has control over his choices, he then acts like a trapped animal, and is disrespectful and makes irresponsible choices.

A win-win experience is where you and your teen feel good about your interactions. Each of you feels that one's own voice is being heard. You both feel respected. To be respected by his parent, to feel heard helps a teenager feel trusted. He learns to make responsible choices and be a trustworthy human being. A teenager who feels he is being viewed as trustworthy then views himself as a trustworthy human being. He makes choices based on that view of his own self. As the parent, you must find opportunities to help your teen realize that you feel he can be trusted.

Depending on your teenager's personality and your history with him, you must consider where you can begin to explore opportunities to catch your teen in the act of being trustworthy. In what situations can you talk with your teen about the notion that you trust him to be respectful and make responsible choices? What do you do if there have been multiple examples of the opposite?

No matter what your teen may be saying, it is imperative that you try to learn what his voice actually is. Although there are unique qualities among teens, and each teen is an individual and must be treated as such, there are certain key themes among teens. Increasing your knowledge of these themes can help you understand your teen's voice. Among others, the following are several of the key and common themes: the struggle between being independent and dependent, feeling like your parent does not understand you, feeling like your parent does not trust you, wanting to feel respected, and adjusting to the emotional and physical changes being a teenager brings.

As mentioned above, one key theme among teens is that typically they want to feel that they are making independent choices. Within that, they want to feel responsible, be trusted, not be told what to do, yet still be helped or guided when they need it. They want to be treated as a young adult in many instances, but like a kid in other instances.

If you recognize this theme, then you recognize that when your teen is frustrated and acting disrespectfully, the problem may very well be that he feels his voice is not being heard. The solution to the problem may be that you must prove to your teenager that you do hear his voice by admitting that you may not have heard it before. Admitting that does not show weakness, nor does it create a manipulative teen. Acknowledging that you may not have heard his voice before but you want to hear it now helps your teen feel heard. Typically, teens believe that their parents do not understand anything they are saying or going through. Your admittance will validate their already existing belief system, and let them know of your desire to work with them.

Look again at the five-step process addressed in this chapter under the elementary and middle school section. You may incorporate that process with your teen. Next is an additional step-by-step process that can also help you achieve the goal of hearing your teen's voice in particular.

Step #1. *Try to find out what your teenager's voice may be.*

His voice includes what he is thinking and feeling, what he might have said and might not have said, whether he has clearly articulated what is on his mind. Try to read between the lines. Try to read what his voice is saying from his actions. The way to do this is to remember and consider the key themes given above, and ask yourself what is on your teen's mind. If you truly have no clue, that is a big, in-your-face indicator that communication between you and your teen has declined and you are out of touch with what is happening in his world. Do not think you can never develop a relationship with your teen. It just means that you need to try to begin the process of hearing his voice.

Step #2. *At an appropriate time, discuss with your teenager where you have been amiss, and express your desire to correct that.*

Consider where you have been amiss as it relates to common teen themes. Specifically, the key to step #2 is communicating to your teen that you recognize that he is becoming a young man and is not a young child anymore. Explain to your teen that you hope to work as a teammate with him on parenting a child that is becoming a young man. Focus on the point that you feel you have been lacking in recognizing that he is in the next phase of his life, but not because you do not care. You care greatly about him. You love him greatly. You value him greatly. Express just as he is adjusting to the changes he is experiencing on the journey of childhood to manhood, you are also adjusting.

An appropriate time to have this discussion is *not* when you are in the middle of an argument. An appropriate time is *not* as your teen is walking through the door after the curfew. An appropriate time *is* when your teenager is willing to have a discussion with you, and you are in a fairly calm mood. I have found that when it comes to most teenagers, the best time to talk is when you are in the car on the way to the store to buy something for him (e.g. his shampoo, jeans). There are other appropriate times, of course. Many parents find that sitting down to dinner together is a good time. However, more often than not, especially if there is already a strained relationship, talking in the car is a useful time to speak with teenagers. There is nowhere else your teen "needs" to go. And you are on your way doing something for him, which increases the positive nature of the encounter.

Contrary to popular belief, there are many examples of things a parent can do with a teenager that provides for an environment to talk. I recall one mother who began taking power walks with her teenage son after months of having a strained relationship. This was very helpful in reconnecting because they were doing something they both enjoyed. After a few weeks of power walking together, they began talking more, and reconnecting as parent and teenager. I also recall a father and his son hitting golf balls together. Some other examples include; a mother and daughter walking in the mall together looking at clothes, a father and daughter bowling, a father and son fishing together, and a parent and child going to a restaurant.

Step #3. *Ask your child to please help you on your quest to interact with him in a more positive and productive way. Ask him to help you to achieve this shift you are trying to make.*

Indeed, you began step #3 during step #2. Now is when you attend to this notion further. A teenager can absolutely understand this notion. Explain that you are trying to hear his voice. Tell him what you think he might be thinking *and* what you are thinking. Do not forget to ask him if you understand a piece of what is on his mind, or do you not understand him at all. In this way, if you say something accurate, you are validating his already-existing feelings, which means you are hearing his voice and opening up the opportunity for him to speak. You are also helping him to hear your voice. You can ask if you are accurate in your assumptions. Say that you sincerely want to understand what he is thinking. You can find out if you are wrong and do not understand what he is saying. If you understand something, but not everything, ask him to explain. Tell him that you are interested in his view on how this situation can be resolved.

Step #4. *Engage in a dialogue to confirm comprehension and experience validation for both of you.*

Validate his voice by repeating what he says. Then restate your view. You can do this concisely, almost in a list with bullets. It should be clear, to the point, and comprehensive. Confirm with your teen whether or not you "get it."

Step #5. *Now that you each hear where the other is coming from, discuss your desire to figure out how you can make a new arrangement that will satisfy both your needs because the opinions of both of you are of equal importance.*

Do you notice the ongoing weave of technique with parenting philosophy? Step #5 is the development of a solution as a team. This reinforces the Dr. Karen Parenting Philosophy, and applies Technique #1 to your family. Step #5 allows for brainstorming and planning as a parent-teen unit, where the teen feels a part of the solution.

Step #6 has components A, B, and C as follows:

A. State that you are glad that you were able to come together as a young adult and parent, and that you look forward to trying out the plan that you created as a team.

B. State that you know if you and he work together, you will both be successful.

C. Implement a check-in plan. Ask your teenager what he thinks about the idea of checking in with each other next week to see how your new plan is working for both of you. Explain that this might be a good idea so that what is working can keep working, and if something is not working, you can tweak the idea together.

Now that you have read the step-by-step process

focusing on teens, let us examine the scenario of the fourteen-year-old in the six steps to see how the process works.

Step #1. Ask yourself, "Self, what do I think my teen is feeling and thinking?" Through his angry response directed at you, a teen is typically saying, "Mom, I am sick and tired of you not cutting me some slack around here." He may also be saying, "You treat me like I am a baby. I am not a baby anymore. I need to decide where I am going without feeling like you always have to know exactly where I am going, like I can't think for myself. You must think I am stupid or something." He may also be saying, "That curfew is like I am ten years old. You must not trust me. You must think I am going to do something stupid if I am out late. You don't know me at all."

Okay, parents, this is what your teen may be thinking. Let's go to the next step.

Step #2. Ask your teenager if there is something that he needs or wants to get from the store this week. Say that you will make the time to take him there so he can get it. When in the car, speak to your teen. "I recognize that you are getting older and becoming a young man. I was thinking, perhaps I have not recognized that. I think I missed when you got older. That is my mistake. I want to recognize that perhaps your needs have changed. I have noticed that each time I ask you where you are going, you get pretty frustrated with me for asking. Perhaps that is because you might be feeling that I don't trust your choices. If that is what you have been thinking, I am sorry that my actions have led you to think that. On the contrary, I do trust that you have the knowledge, skills, and ability to make wise and responsible choices."

You can go on to explain that when you ask your teenager where he is going, it says more about where you are in your development than where he is. "You see," you can say, "I love you so much that I worry when you are out. Not because I don't trust you! It's because you have grown up so fast, and I am trying to get used to that and adjust to the fact that I can't protect you all of the time. I guess if I know where you are, and who you are with, and I know you will be home not too late, I feel safer. It makes me feel like I can somehow protect you. But I realize I can't. Knowing where you are gives me a sense of inner calm. When you were younger, I was often with you, but not anymore. So please forgive me if you feel that I have been treating you like a baby by wanting to know where you are and setting a curfew. It is not my intention to be disrespectful. It is really just that I get nervous about others in the world that I cannot control. I know I cannot control you. I really don't want to. I trust in you." Continue in this vein. "With the trust I have in you, because we are on the same team, I know that if I did not specifically ask you where you are going, you would just tell me because you know that part of having a healthy adult relationship is one adult telling the other adult where they are going. I tell Dad, and Dad tells me where he is going."

Tailor this conversation to fit your unique situation. I offer you this example as an outline upon which to build your conversation.

Step #3. Say to your teen, "I totally need your help with how I can shift to being the parent of a teenager. I have ideas about what you may be thinking and what I can do differently, but of course, I don't know all your thoughts. Can I share with you what I think is going on? Will you tell me where I get it and where I am missing the boat?" Wait for your teen to say okay, then continue. "I was thinking about how I can be less on top of you because perhaps you feel suffocated by my needing to know everything. Perhaps you can feel more like a young adult. I must admit that I can try not being so nervous. Perhaps you would be willing to help me with incorporating who you are now into our lives. I recognize that you are more independent, but also at times still need my help." Then ask your teen, "Was any of that right or am I totally off base?" Based on your teen's answer, explain that you really want to understand so you can make the shift from parent-child relationship, to teammates that are parent-young adult.

Step #4. Say to your teen, "If I understand you correctly, you feel I am treating you like a baby. You feel I am showing you that I don't trust you and don't understand you by:

1. Asking you where you are going.

2. Asking who you are going with.

3. Setting a curfew that is too early.

"From my point of view," you continue:

1. I do trust you.

2. I do want to know where you are going and who with, but not because I am trying to police you. As a *family team,* we all should know where other family members are and who they are with.

3. I realize that our family team needs to discuss a curfew that you feel makes sense based on your stage of life."

Step #5. Continue the discussion. "Now that we both understand where each other is coming from, I am sure that we can work together as a team so that we can both feel our needs are met. How about if we take turns expressing our ideas and figuring out a compromise?" Ask your teen for his opinion about a curfew. Then say, "Okay, so you think your curfew should be midnight, I think ten o'clock. Would closer to your time, but a little earlier, be okay? How about 11:30? And then next month, we can talk again and see if that is working, okay?"

Continue your discussion. "As for the other point we are looking at, specifically, that I like to know where you are going and who you are going with, let's figure out what to do. I really want you to feel that I trust you, so I will do my best not to make you feel like I am interrogating you. I feel more comfortable just knowing where you are and perhaps which of your friends you will be with." Ask your teenager what ideas he has for this issue. Suggest that perhaps he will just tell you now that he knows it is not because you want to control him or do not trust him, but because it makes you feel safe, and you love him.

Now that the key reasons why he did not share with you where he was going and who with have been taken out of the game, he may no longer hold onto his need to withhold information. Now that he understands where you are coming from and feels you understand where he is coming from, and that you are sincere about your desire to work with him, his actions may shift. This is what typically happens. Typically, when a parent incorporates the notion of hearing her teen's voice, the teen feels heard. That, in and of itself, helps a positive shift to occur. The teen's problematic disrespectful and/or irresponsible behavior ceases to exist because now his voice is being heard.

Step #6. See the three components as written previously for Step #6 and implement.

CHAPTER 4

TECHNIQUE #2: UNDERSTAND THAT ALL BEHAVIORS MAKE SENSE IN CONTEXT. TAKE AWAY THE CONTEXT

During my Masters program, I recall reading about a research project undertaken by Gregory Bateson, Don D. Jackson, Jay Haley, and John H. Weakland, where a theory of schizophrenia was looked at. In *Steps to an Ecology of Mind*, Gregory Bateson discusses the result of that research project. The theory suggests that schizophrenic behaviors "make sense" when viewed within the context of one's family. In other words, we do not exist in a vacuum. Our behaviors are learned and are not developed in isolation. Rather, our behaviors develop as a result of our interactions. We learn to act within a given context, and it is within that context that our behaviors make sense. As asserted by Bill O'Hanlon and James Wilk in *Shifting Contexts*, to terminate any pattern, all that is needed is to transform the context.

The idea that all behaviors make sense in context may sound quite odd, at first hearing. You may ask, "How can all behaviors make sense?" You may follow that question with an example of an action your child displayed that leads you to say, "That behavior made absolutely no sense." It is when you believe that your child's behavior makes no sense that you are likely to say or do something that does not help solve that problem. If you cannot see how your child's behavior makes sense, then the solution you develop will come from your lack of understanding. This often leads to an exacerbation of the problem.

If you can recognize that your child is adjusting to something, then you can try to uncover what he is adjusting to. Then you are able to make sense of his behavior, thus you can take away/transform the context.

The following examples show how to use Technique #2 to help your child become more respectful and responsible.

PRESCHOOLERS

Picture a scenario where a four-year-old boy named Scott is having a life-changing experience. He now has a baby sister. That is an event to adjust to. The parents are hearing the "big brother" talking in a baby voice, which he has not done before. For example, when you ask him to pick out which shirt he would like to wear to school, rather than picking it out as he has been doing for the past few months, he now says in a baby voice, "I don't wanna. I don't know what I wanna wear, I cannnnnn't." When you tell him it is his responsibility to pick out his shirt, he replies, "Noooooo, I won't do it. You do it, or else I'll _____ [fill in the blank with undesirable behavior]." The threats go on for a number of days. He comes up with various threats, including, "I'll put cream cheese on your nose," "I will mush applesauce on my head," "I will take all of the paper cups out of the cabinet and throw them on the floor."

As the parent, you may become frustrated and feel that your child is being disrespectful to you, as well as being irresponsible in not taking care of his morning responsibility. You also notice he is not being respectful to his baby sister. For an example, you ask him to stop pushing the baby carrier when the baby is in it while you are getting everything else ready to go out. You explain that it makes his baby sister scared. This is being very disrespectful to her. You also say that what he is doing is being irresponsible because it is dangerous, and as the big brother, he should act more responsibly.

Try to use Technique #2 here to create a solution. Remind yourself that adjustment is typically why behavioral problems emerge. The solution is to understand how the behavior makes sense; remember, the behavior is just a symptom of the problem, not the actual problem. Yes, the symptom of the problem can become the problem, so now it is time to understand what the context is. When you figure out what the context is, then you will be able to figure out how to take it away.

The context in this situation is that the boy was the "king fish" prior to his sister's birth. Now he feels second best. He felt like he was "top dog," but that is no longer true. Rather than feeling special, he no longer feels special. Before the birth of his sister, he got all of the attention, but now he has to share your attention. His seemingly disrespectful and irresponsible behavior is a symptom of the problem, not the actual problem (the context), but it has become the presenting problem.

At first glance, you might often wonder if the problem is the birth of the second child. No, that is not the problem or the context; the problem/context is the fact that he is feeling diminished. If the problem (him feeling less than) is removed, then the problem behavior (disrespectful and irresponsible behavior) will cease to exist.

Now you can ask yourself, "How do I get rid of the problem?" The context/problem is not always what it appears to be. The context/problem in this example appears to be the birth of a second child, but if we always see the context as what appears to be the cause of the problem, it will be hard to figure out how to do away with the context. In this example, getting rid of the second child is not the right solution! The context/problem is how your son is feeling about himself. He has had this feeling since the birth of his sister. Therefore, the solution needs to be to help him shift his view of himself. This is getting rid of the context. The solution is to help the big brother feel just as special and important as he did before. When you help your son to shift his thinking, then his thinking of himself as "less than" will cease to exist.

Let's look at another example. Visualize a scenario where your three-year-old son, Nick, wants to eat a hot dog for dinner. He ate one last night, and you do not want to give him a hot dog two nights in a row because you feel that eating them often is not a healthy eating habit. When you tell him no, however, he gets very irate and yells that he wants it *now*. You reply to him, "Don't you raise your voice at me. I am the parent and I said no. And what I say goes." Nick says, "If you don't give me a hot dog, I am going to chop you up into pieces and put you in the garbage pail!"

If you see this as disrespectful behavior, how you

respond may be different than if you see it as a matter of adjustment. Parents will say a variety of things that this clinician recommends against using if they see their young children as being disrespectful. "No dinner for you. Go to your room." "How dare you say that to me? Take this plate of broccoli and eat it now, or else you are not going on your play date tomorrow." "You are so disrespectful. Just for that, I am taking away your stuffed animal, and you can have it back when you learn to speak without a dirty mouth." None of the aforementioned responses fit the Dr. Karen Parenting Philosophy, nor is it an example of implementing technique #2. None of these responses help resolve the problem, nor do they address the symptoms of the problem. None of these responses show a parent trying to understand the child's behavior and generating a solution. None of these responses are helpful communications. None of these responses resolve or teach a child anything. They certainly do not help the child act respectfully or responsibly the next time he is faced with a situation where someone tells him no to something that he wants.

There are options. Let us try Technique #2. Ask yourself, what might this child be adjusting to? Consider Nick's age, his stage of development. Perhaps Nick is discovering that there are things he can be in charge of, in control of, make his own decisions about, and there are also things he does not get to control. This discovery is challenging for him. He is struggling with it. When you decide what he eats, this makes him feel out of control of his own little world. You made it clear that you are in charge, that you are the boss. Perhaps he was in the mood to be in charge that night. Perhaps thirty minutes later, when you ask him to put on his pajamas all by himself, he is not feeling so independent and wants your help, but at suppertime, he was feeling independent.

Now that you have made your hypothesis about what your child may be trying to adjust to, being in control versus not being in control, you can make sense of Nick's behavior. You say to yourself, "If he chops me up and puts me in the garbage pail, that will get me out of his way. If I am out of the picture, so to speak, then of course he is free to be in control and in charge, to be the boss and decide what he wants to eat. And if he wants to eat ten hot dogs and five chocolate bars, that is what he will do." You have made sense of his behavior, and the window of opportunity is here for you to help your child understand why he said what he did. You can help him learn about his thoughts and personal challenges. This will help him be respectful and make responsible choices. You can help him learn to cope with challenges when he feels like his opinion is not being recognized.

At this point, you can say something like this, "Oh, honey, I know you really enjoy hot dogs, which is exactly why you ate one last night. And I know your tongue is saying, 'Yummy! Hotdogs! I want one.' But I need to be a good mommy because I love you. It is my responsibility to make sure I help you learn healthy eating habits so that way your belly and brain says, 'Thank you, Nick, I love the choices you make to feed me.' I don't want your belly to say, 'Oh, Nick, I hurt. That was too many hot dogs.' Now I know that you love me and don't really want to chop me up and put me in the garbage pail. Did you just say that because that was your way of trying to get me out of the way so you can have a hot dog?" When Nick says yes, you continue. "Oh, honey, you can tell me how you feel without saying something like that. You know, you can say that you are disappointed because you want to eat a hot dog. You can always tell me when you disagree with me, whatever the topic is, okay? So, honey, does it make you feel angry that I was telling you what to eat?" Nick says yes, and now you can say, "Oh, Nick, you can tell me that. Tell me it makes you feel angry when you do not get to choose. It must be hard when there are things you are in charge of, and then there are things you are not, huh?"

After you listen to his response, explain that he can often be in charge of what he eats. Explain that you know he has a smart and healthy brain and that if he chooses to listen to his brain instead of his tongue, his brain will help him make a more responsible choice about what to eat. Then ask him to try it. Ask him what his brain's idea is. Also, ask him what his belly's idea is. Ask him what his tongue's idea is. Ask him, if different parts of his body could talk, would each part of his body say different things? Ask him if sometimes different parts of his body agree, and other times disagree. Ask him which part of his body he should listen to if he wants to make a responsible choice for his belly. Should he listen to his brain or his tongue? Communicate to your child you are always interested in how he feels, and in his opinion. Verbalize to him that you hope he will always feel comfortable and be willing to tell you how he feels.

In this example, many positive things can happen if you open your mind to the notion expressed in Technique #2.

You can see in this example that you can take away the parent-child power struggle and replace it with respectful conversation. You are also using Technique #1 by treating your child with respect and hearing his voice, valuing his opinion, and teaching him how to express his thoughts in a respectful way. You have also helped him increase his self-awareness, and helped him to learn to use his voice in a respectful manner that gets heard. By using Technique #2, making sense of his behavior, you took away the context! By explaining to him that his brain knows the responsible choice, and he can choose to listen to his brain, you put him back in charge. This is a fine example of driving home the point that you can help your children learn how to express themselves in a positive and productive manner, and thus be respectful and make responsible choices.

TEENAGERS

Imagine the following scenario: A thirteen-year-old girl has an eating disorder. Her mother is trying to resolve this eating disorder. It is the mother's belief that the daughter is disrespecting her body and making an irresponsible choice. The mother does not mean harm, but she thinks that by trying to control her daughter's eating, the problem will be resolved. Specifically, when she sees her daughter not eating as much as she thinks she should, the mother stands over her and tells her, "You have to eat." Like many teenagers, this girl has been trying but struggling to adjust to being independent and making her own choices. She wants to experience a sense of control in her own world. Teenagers often struggle with trying to understand the notion of what is within human control and what is not. This is part of a teenager's adjustment.

This particular teenager has a history of enjoying experimenting with her body. For an example, she often experiments with coloring her hair with store-purchased dyes and cutting her hair on her own. She enjoys trying different color nail polish each week. She has painted her own t-shirts to make her own styles to wear. The teen stated that before her eating disorder began, she had heard her mother make negative comments to her directly and to others, about her personality. The girl said that the choices she was making (e.g., hair, nail polish, clothes) she believes fell into the category of individual choice, but her mother always tried to control her and put a stop to her explorations. In the girl's opinion, she was making positive choices on her own, which was part of her adjustment process. Rather than feeling supported by her mother, she said that her mother's style of parenting was consistently controlling and negative. She did not feel in control of her own self. The girl also reported her memory of when she wanted to pierce her ears, and the mother said, "No. It isn't your body until you are eighteen years old." Instilling in your child that she has no control and cannot make her own choices about her body until she is eighteen creates a child who is not responsible.

Helping the mother to understand that her daughter is trying to adjust to what is *in* her control and what is *out* of her control is important. The mother needed to understand that her daughter wanted to experience control within her world. If the girl had the opportunity to explore control in a healthy manner, this could significantly help this family. At this point, the mother could potentially understand how her daughter's behavior made sense in the context of exploring the notion of control. This was a situation where a thirteen-year-old girl felt like she had no control (the context), so she decided that she would control what she did with her body. If her world became less controlled by her mother, then her behavior might change because the context had changed.

It is important for a teenage girl to feel that she can make choices about her body, and other things in her life. If a girl feels she has no choices about anything in her world, she will focus on trying to control aspects of her body, for her body is the one thing that truly is hers. In this case, however, the mother was even stifling that by saying the girl's body was not hers until the age of eighteen.

People often think therapists blame parents for all problems. However, it is absolutely *not* my intention, nor is it my theoretical belief system that a parent is to be blamed for every problem that exists. There are, of course, disorders a person may be predisposed to, based on biology and not environmental upbringing (i.e., what a parent said or did not say to her child). In any case example, whether or not the person has a biological predisposition, we cannot deny that the choices parents make can and do affect one's children.

The key is to create a solution where the context; mom in control, daughter with no control, ceases to exist. The goal is to take away the context and then the girl will feel some control of her world. Then the symptom of the problem (eating disorder) ceases to exist. This is a fine example of where the mother can absolutely play a role in helping her daughter.

Consider the fourteen-year-old boy discussed in the previous chapter. Once his parent heard his voice (which validated and supported his feelings), the context no longer existed. The context was that the boy felt like he was being treated like a baby, which led to a power struggle. Once this context no longer existed, the problem of disrespectful behavior no longer had to exist. In this scenario, the outcome was that the teen started coming home on time, and told his mother more often who he was going out with and where he was going.

CHAPTER 5

TECHNIQUE #3: REFRAME POSITIVELY

There are times when one of the first two techniques in applying the Dr. Karen Parenting Philosophy are the best to use, there are other times when implementing both is the most appropriate. There may be other times when a different technique or blend of techniques will work best. Technique #3 is positive reframing. One of the interesting things about this reframing technique is that it is similar to making sense of behavior. But it is also different.

Reframing is similar to making sense of behavior in that reframing allows a situation to be viewed in a different way. Reframing is different in that you are not taking away/transforming the context; rather, you are *labeling* your child's behavior in a new and different way. Reframing has its own unique style. Not only is this technique about considering how you see your child's behavior, it is also about how you are labeling your child's behavior more positively. Label what your child is doing with different words.

INFANTS

The following is an example of using Technique #3. An infant is crying. If you consider crying as manipulative behavior the baby uses to get what she wants, then you are framing your infant as a manipulator. This frame, or point of view, informs you of further choices you make in your style of parenting. Your choices can also validate an already existing parenting philosophy. For example, you might say, "My baby will not learn self-reliance if I go in to attend to her each time she cries. She will not self-soothe." The philosophy that the baby needs to work it out on her own quite clearly means you are not going to hear her voice and treat her voice as important.

In contrast, when you reframe positively, you can view the infant's behavior as "smart." This frame informs you on how to behave and, of course, helps develop or validate your parenting philosophy. Specifically, you can say, "When I am respectful to my baby's voice, I am being a responsible parent. My baby learns that she can rely on me to come to her aid when she calls. My baby will learn from her own experience of being treated with respect how to relate to others respectfully and responsibly. She will grow to be a child and then an adult who is respectful and responsible."

Positive reframing will allow you to say, "Ah, what a wise baby. She has figured out how to get her needs met." You believe that your child is learning that when you come to her aid, she will feel special. She will learn in infancy that she is important, she matters, she is a valued person, and her voice counts. That will affect her view of herself as someone who deserves respect. The web effect will affect her and the choices she makes throughout her life. Being respectful of this infant's needs thus creates a child who is respectful of you and your needs. She will learn to treat herself and others respectfully, and to make responsible choices. You heard her voice. She will hear hers, yours, and others.

PRESCHOOLER/ELEMENTARY

Let us use another example, a six-year-old child who is hesitant to stay at his friend's house for a play date without his mother. He may be labeled as a nervous child; he may be labeled as having separation anxiety. These terms may then be used in other contexts. For example, on a school field trip, the children are driven to and from school by parent volunteers. The child is comfortable riding in Dan's car, but not in Amy's car. You say, "you are such a Nervous Nelly," or in your frustration, you may say mean and hurtful things, like, "Cut the cord, already," (meaning cut the umbilical cord). When you label a child, be careful what label you use. The frame you are placing around your child is what he may walk around with for the rest of his life.

Imagine a picture frame around your child's face with the label on the frame. If you do not like the label, if it is a derogatory label, then put a different frame around that child. Make a different label. When you reframe your child's behavior, this reframes your child's view of himself and other people's views of him, too. When you reframe your view of your child and see him positively, you are considering the notion that a behavior can be seen in a variety of ways. The way you see the behavior has everything to do with the label you choose, or the frame you place around the child

In the example given above, you do not want your child

to be trapped in this "nervous kid" label. When the window of opportunity opens for him to be more comfortable in new situations, you do not want him to feel trapped by a label. The interesting thing about labels is that it is often derived from an actual, noticeable, consistent behavior. Indeed, there may be truth to the so-called negative label. It is important to be aware of a child's consistent behavioral pattern. If that is the case, you need to notice its consistency and recognize it for what it is. You do not want to be blind and think everything is wonderful with your kid, and not try to get help when help is needed. It is imperative that you recognize the behavior for what it is, e.g., nervous or anxious. But you must recognize that the label is *not* the full story. This means you do not want to define your child's whole being by that one character trait.

If you label a child, he becomes generally defined by that label. Then his view of himself becomes the label, and others start seeing him as that label. When key players in the child's life begin to view a particular behavior as his personality trait, this could lead to the label "dysfunctional." Our views of ourselves are directly connected to whether we act responsibly and respectfully, or not.

Try Technique #3 with the example given above. Give the so-called nervous child, the child with separation anxiety, a positive reframe such as "cautious, conscious child." Reinforce this new label with a statement that supports it. For an example, consider the notion that this child has an older awareness. At a very young age, he is wise beyond his years and recognizes that we have to be cautious about who we trust in this world because not

everybody is going to look out for us. Because he is only six, however, he cannot always evaluate and distinguish who he can trust. Therefore, he wants his parent to be there while he investigates the situation until he decides whether it is an okay or not-okay environment for him to be in without his parent. This child is safety-conscious and wants to use his own eyes and ears to see if these other people are indeed trustworthy. By reframing this child as cautious and having an older awareness, you help him to be seen in a positive way by others.

By following your child's comfort level, and letting him be cautious, he can see himself more positively and grow from caution to comfort. As he gets older, he will feel confidence in himself that he can evaluate situations and determine if it will be wise and safe to engage in. You are teaching your child to trust in his inner voice, and therefore he will be a person that makes responsible choices.

With your positive reframing, you have actually helped your child to be ready to enter the next phase of development, which might be to stay at a friend's house for a play date without you. As a child, he may not always judge accurately, or see what you see. With a play date, perhaps you feel the location is safe, but your child is developing his own judgment skills, and you can help him along by respecting his opinion. Can you see the general applications of the Dr. Karen Parenting Philosophy? Do you see the techniques as intertwined? Treat your child as an equal member of the family (the Dr. Karen Parenting Philosophy). Hear his voice (Technique #1). Try to understand how his behavior makes sense (Technique #2). You are not taking away the context as you work with the

technique that all behavior makes sense in context; rather, you are viewing his behavior through a positive lens (Technique #3). Thus, you are positively reframing.

You can also view your child as adjusting. You can discuss with him how you understand he is still adjusting to the idea of going into another child's car, or going to a friend's house without you. Letting your child know that you know he is working on feeling comfortable, that he is adjusting to new ideas makes him feel like he will eventually adjust.

Furthermore, discuss with your six-year-old that you are impressed that he takes the time to evaluate situations before he acts; tell him it is a very impressive quality. Explore with this child that he has a think-before-act life philosophy rather than acting impulsively. Discuss that it is quite a skill to have at a young age and that it will take him far in life in a variety of contexts. Impulsivity is a negative character trait that gets people into trouble. Telling him this is certainly giving him a healthier self-image, and it gives him the opportunity to develop a positive label in contrast to a negative one. This trait and skill of thinking before acting helps a child to make responsible choices. Often, impulsive choices can be irresponsible.

Chapter 6

Technique #4: Keep The Theme Of Positive Style Of Interaction: The Big Three

If your child consistently experiences that you believe he is a responsible child, the odds that he will act responsibly because he now views himself as responsible increase tremendously. If you treat your child respectfully, your child will believe he is deserving of respectful treatment, which means he believes that he must be a respectful human being. Therefore, the odds increase greatly for your child to act respectfully. It is this very positive style of interacting that you have with your child that does indeed impact him in his view of self.

When it comes to raising respectful children who make responsible choices, note that children are impacted by their parents' view of them and their parents' belief in them. Children often think they are who their parents think they are, and thus act as such. Therefore, it is imperative that you *keep the theme of positive style of interaction* with the three types of communication. I refer to this as the Big Three: verbal expression, body language, and physical expression. This chapter will clarify the differences between each piece of the Big Three.

Each of the three ways of communicating is beautiful

and important in its own right, and when all three are consistently used together in your interactions with your children, they have a powerful affect on the development of your children's thoughts and actions. Your intent is to help your child feel true positive interaction coming from you. Including the Big Three in your parenting style helps your child feel respected, and a child who feels respected also feels valued and important. Feeling respected leads the child to feel worthy of respect, and he may say to himself, "If my parents are being respectful to me, then I must be a special person who is worthy of respect. I must be respectful as a human being if I am being treated respectfully." This is a child who desires to make responsible decisions.

Keeping to the theme of a positive style of interaction in terms of your verbal interaction, your body language, and how you relate to your child with physical expressions is just what it sounds like. Here is an example of the positive style of interaction using the Big Three. If your child is telling you about his day, stop what you are doing (body language). For an example, close the magazine you are reading or put away your laptop. Show your child that you are paying attention by acknowledging his words, repeating back certain key words or sentences, and asking questions (verbal expression). In addition, perhaps you can give him a hug during or at the end of the conversation, or maybe you can pat him on the back, or give his cheek a gentle caress (physical expression).

To clarify Technique #4, the following is the Big Three broken down as follows:

1. VERBAL EXPRESSION

Using your verbal skills as a parent means using words concretely. For example, you can say, "I am proud of you." Make positive statements like: "I feel so blessed to have you as my son," "I love you so very much," "You are so precious," and "You are so special." These statements are positive and keep your interaction positive; even when there are challenging days and moments never withhold love. The idea is to use clear and concrete words and speak in a positive manner.

When you are talking with your child and repeating what he says, you are using a reflective style of communication. That helps ensure that you hear what he says and that he feels heard. It is also important to ask questions with interest, not as an interrogator. Having a nice selection of vocal tones is also helpful. A monotone voice conveys lack of interest.

2. BODY LANGUAGE

Nonverbal body language means using your body as a method of communicating. Your body says a lot; when you are smiling, jumping for joy, clapping your hands, closing the book you are reading, turning off the television show you are watching, putting aside the email you are reading, raising your arms enthusiastically, giving a thumbs-up gesture, looking directly into your child's eyes when he is speaking to you, and facing him when he speaks.

3. PHYSICAL EXPRESSION

Physical expression is using touch with your child. You can, for example, hug your child. Some authorities suggest, depending on the age and gender of your child, that you need to stop being physically affectionate with your child. This clinician completely disagrees with this. It is imperative to express yourself in a loving, nurturing, physical way with your child, no matter what the age and gender. There is a belief that if you hug your son too much, he will become a "wuss." When I hear popular personalities on talk shows trying to educate fathers and mothers with this approach, I feel so sad for the child. Whether your child is a boy or a girl, physical affection helps them to develop a sense of wholeness and a love of self and others. A child who receives physical affection feels deserving of receiving love, and thus wants to continue to receive love and give it back. This is a child who is respectful to himself and others, and makes responsible choices. He feels good within. For example, a fourteen-year-old boy will still benefit from hugs. In fact, a thirty-year-old man still benefits from a hug from his dad and mom now and again, and a fifty-five-year-old man also benefits from the nurturing hug of his eighty-five-year-old father and eighty-three-year-old mother. Such a hug is very manly.

Wanting to receive and give love is a wonderful desire that instills a feeling of completeness in a human being. If a person feels valued and loved, he also feels worthy of receiving love and respect, and therefore is respectful to others and makes responsible choices. Examples of physical expression include handholding, patting someone on the back, touching the other person's arm, caressing a cheek, and kissing.

Technique #4, keeping a positive style of interacting with your child, is how you want to define your relationship. You do not want the challenging moments to define your relationship, as the challenges are only some moments in time. A child who feels positive in his sense of the parent-child relationship feels *whole,* and not like there is a hole inside him waiting to be filled. This is the child who feels good inside and has much to offer to himself and others. Acting respectfully and responsibly come naturally to a child who feels nourished by his parents who consistently use the Big Three.

A great example of utilizing the Big Three is expressing to your child that you are proud of him.

It is the Dr. Karen belief that you tell your child that you are proud of him in words and through body language and physical expression often.

When you use all three means of communication, your child knows that you feel proud of him.

Let us look at the following example: your eight-year-old daughter, Irena, tells you that her friends, Geri and Sharon, have been excluding her lately, but that it is really Sharon who is causing this problem. You spend time discussing some options with Irena and try to help her solve the problem. She tells you that she will try to talk with Sharon. The next day, or perhaps a few days later, your daughter comes home from school and tells you that at lunchtime, she talked with Sharon about her feelings and was hoping that Sharon would include her again. Sharon said that she would. This is a big deal in your daughter's life. You can reinforce her method of communication by using Technique #4, with the specific focus on how proud you are of her.

As the above example shows, the Dr. Karen Parenting Philosophy is not just to incorporate the nine techniques when your child is acting disrespectful or irresponsible. The Dr. Karen Parenting Philosophy is a way of life. It is a daily parenting philosophy that determines how you relate to your child. When you interact with your child in a positive way when there is a problem behavior, as well as when your child is displaying behavior that you are proud of, this helps develop who your child becomes. When implementing the Dr. Karen Parenting Philosophy with consistency, you will discover that your child will not need to be disciplined for poor choices, irresponsible behavior, or disrespectful behavior.

Let's look further at this example. Your daughter, Irena, has come home and told you about the outcome at school. It is important not to just say, "Good. I am glad that you and Sharon are friends again." The important point is not just that they are friends again; the point to focus on is that your daughter confronted the situation and solved the problem in a very healthy way. Your goal is to reinforce the idea of positive problem resolution. Your response should be along the following lines: "I am so proud of you for discussing the problem the two of you were having, and really trying to work on a resolution with your friend." Along with your verbal expression of being proud, give your daughter a smile and a hug. The smile is the nonverbal communication, and the hug is the physical communication.

So often, people express their belief that if you say you

are proud too often, it will have a negative effect on children. The Dr. Karen Parenting Philosophy holds the view that expressing your pride in your child is not only important, it is imperative. It does *not* have a negative impact. It is truly positive, both for the short-term and the long-term in the development of a respectful and responsible child.

Take the time right now to consider an event that has occurred with your child where you could consider using Technique #4. The following is an example of utilizing the Big Three, along with the theme of being proud of your child in a three-step form:

Step #1. Say, "I am proud of you because _____ [fill in the blank]."

Step #2. While saying the above, or after you say those words, give a body language response. For an example, smile and/or give a thumbs-up.

Step #3. Then engage in a physical interaction. For an example, give your child a hug, pat her back, or give her a high five.

Now let's look at how to apply the concept of being proud by using the Big Three, even when your child has not displayed an action to be proud of, or even when a child has not done something that you feel warrants a positive style of interaction. Keeping the theme of a positive style of interaction is necessary rather than a common parenting method response of taking disciplinary action. When you keep a positive style of interaction in challenging times, you can use the challenge as an opportunity to help your child develop into a respectful person who makes responsible choices. Does punishment help develop a child who is respectful or responsible at his core? Dr. Karen's answer to this question is no.

When something happens that you are not proud of, it is important that you incorporate the Big Three along with a two-part verbalization (i.e., two steps) to incorporate Dr. Karen's Proud, Planting Seeds technique. Your statement would include the following:

Step #1. Say, "I am not proud of that choice that you made to _____ [fill in the blank with the irresponsible or disrespectful behavior]." Your facial expression should show disappointment. Your hand may be gently placed on your child's shoulder. Notice the utilization of the Big Three.

Then ask, "Are you proud of that behavior?" Your child answers the question. He may say no, shake his head, lower his head down, or sigh. Whatever the response is, it is one that shows your child recognizes that it was not a good choice. Perhaps your child may try to justify his actions rather than admitting he did wrong. If that is the case, be patient and use Technique #1, which is to hear your child's voice. Once you have incorporated Technique #1 and validated his feelings, you may then need to incorporate Technique #2 to find out how it made sense to your child to act the way he did. At this point, notice that your child will be more open for you to apply the Proud, Planting Seeds technique. Continue where you left off and explain that you still are not proud of his actions, though you understand how it made sense to him to act in that way. Discuss with him that *there are other choices.*

Step #2. Say, "The next time you encounter the same situation or a similar one, I will be so proud of you when you choose to _____ [here suggest an alternative choice the child can implement next time]." As you speak, your facial expression is optimistic and your hand goes on his back and rubs gently in a circular motion. Notice the utilization of the Big Three in this two-part verbalization of the incorporation of Dr. Karen's Proud, Planting Seeds technique. Depending on the age and the personality of the child, and perhaps what the actual situation is, impacts whether you fill in the blank for him an alternative behavior. More often than not, even young children can fill in the blank. Make it like you are about to fill in the blank, then say, "Wait. I know *you know* what you can do. What is a different choice you can make?" Then, when your child tells you what the other choice he can make is, use the Big Three to let him know that you have confidence that he will make the responsible and/or respectful choice next time.

Let me say again that the Dr. Karen Parenting Philosophy is not just the incorporation of the techniques when your child is acting disrespectful or irresponsible. *The Dr. Karen Parenting Philosophy is a way of life.* It is a daily parenting philosophy that determines how you relate to your child. By interacting with your child in a positive way when there is problem behavior, as well as when your child is displaying excellent behavior, this guides who your child becomes. Your child will not need to be disciplined for poor choices of irresponsible or disrespectful behavior because he is respectful and responsible.

When incorporating Technique #4, understand, *never*

use negative terminology to refer to your child. It makes him feel negatively labeled. Even seemingly silly nicknames are a definite no-no. A nickname may become a nickname that does not represent who your child is, and yet will become how this child views himself. Therefore, consider wisely what names you call your child. For example, when you call your five-year-old lazy because he does not carry his plate to the sink after dinner, this may become a label he uses to refer to himself in other contexts. Over time, "lazy" will become a part of his self-view. A nickname may also reinforce a behavior that may actually already exist and exacerbate an already existing condition. Using negative terms when referring to your child is dangerous.

Here are just a few examples of names I have heard parents call their children through the years: Piss-ant. Shorty. Goof-ball. Pudgie. Dumb-ass. They also say, "What are you? Stupid? Lazy? A baby?" These names are insulting. Be aware of the message you are giving your child. If you believe your child will not feel good about the person that he becomes if the name you call him is who he is, then do not call him that name. For example, take the name "piss-ant." Ask yourself if you think your child will be likely to live a happy, fulfilling life if he becomes a piss-ant (does this indicate that others piss on him? Literally? Figuratively?). He is little (an ant) and others step on him (piss on him). That does not sound like a pleasant life. A child who feels he is little where others are bigger and can therefore step on him will not be happy in his own skin, and therefore most likely will not reach his full potential. The child that is a "piss-ant" most likely will not develop confidence in his own voice to make responsible and respectful decisions.

It is interesting to consider negative words. If you call your child a name that does not seem to be negative and has no negative connotations, you are making another big mistake if it is not used wisely. For an example, calling your male child "boy" if not used judiciously removes his identify. Saying, "You are such a great boy," "Oh, how I love my wonderful boy," "You are such a big boy," "You are developing into such a fine young man," *is* wonderful. But if instead you often say, "Come on, boy, let's go," or "Boy, did you do your homework?" "Boy, pass the vegetables," "Boy, this" or "Boy, that" and do not use his actual name, he may lose his identity. One's identity is in one's name. If a child hears his name as "boy," then who is he? Who does he think he is? It is fine to call your child a name other than his actual name if it has no negative indications, but it is imperative that you are aware of how often you do this, and in what context.

CHAPTER 7

TECHNIQUE #5: MODEL RESPECTFUL AND RESPONSIBLE BEHAVIOR

When it comes to role modeling, it is this writer's strong belief that what you model in how you relate to your kids, both directly and indirectly in what they observe when you relate to others, impacts your children. Your role modeling has everything to do with their thoughts and actions with regard to relating to themselves and others in a respectful and responsible way.

If I put a dollar in a jar every time I heard a parent shouting out their desire for their child to be respectful, yet they were not being respectful to their child or others, I believe I would be a millionaire. Likewise, if I put a dollar in a jar every time I heard a parent stating their desire for their child to be more responsible, and they themselves were not responsible, again, I would be a millionaire.

This chapter is about looking at yourself in an honest way. The questions in this chapter are designed to first help you look carefully at yourself and consider how you directly relate to your child. Then, you will have the opportunity to consider how you relate to other people and what your child observes.

MODELING RESPECTFUL AND RESPONSIBLE CHOICES IN YOUR INTERACTIONS WITH YOUR CHILD

First, take yourself through the following four questions so that you can be more aware of how you are relating to your child. You can either validate your already existing way of role modeling respect and acting responsibly, or recognize that this is something you need to improve on.

Ask yourself:

1. In my opinion, in what ways do I show that I am respectful to my child each day?

2. If I were looking through my child's eyes, in what ways would she say I show that I respect her each day?

3. In my opinion, in what ways do I show that I act responsibly toward my child each day?

4. If I were looking through my child's eyes, in what ways would she say that I act in a responsible way toward her each day?

If, as you think about the past few days, weeks, and months, you are not sure of the answers to these questions, then I propose a task for you. For the next two to four weeks, ask yourself these questions every day. Your answers will give you a clear understanding of whether you and your child see you as respectful and/or responsible.

Second, ask yourself the four questions again, but focus on the opposite of respectful and responsible. For example, in the first question you would ask yourself: "How do I show that I am *disrespectful* to my child?"

An example of being disrespectful to your child is if you are consistently late to pick your child up from school. You may not see this as irresponsible behavior or being disrespectful to your child, and perhaps you can justify your actions. Perhaps you can make sense of why you are late. (I am sure you can.) For an example, you were running late finishing up your last phone call at work. Perhaps your younger child wanted an extra snack, and that made you late to school. You can make sense of your behavior, especially now that you hold the philosophy that all behaviors make sense in context. Remember, however, that how you make sense of your behavior does not take away the fact that from your child's eyes, it is irresponsible and disrespectful to be late.

Just because you can rationalize your behavior, this does not mean that it is responsible and respectful, or even okay. Your child recognizes that there is a pick-up time and then there is being late. Remember that treating your child as an equal member of the family means treating him in a way that he feels valued, special, and just as important, if not more so than the other responsibilities in your life.

Perhaps your child is not ready in the morning for school and you yell at him for being irresponsible. Or perhaps he has homework, and he seems to often find something else that he says needs to be done first. This often leads to handing in his homework late. Consider this: if you make the shift and model to him that you are responsible by picking him up on time, he may also make a shift and be ready on time in the morning. Perhaps your positive shift will also lead him to do his homework on time.

Imagine a scenario where you ask your child to please take his plate to the sink when he is finished eating. Instead, he leaves it on the table and looks at a magazine. You ask him again, and he says he will do it in a little while. Each time you ask him, he says, "Later." He says he is in the middle of something important. You become more and more frustrated, and the next thing you know, you yell that he is being disrespectful to you. You explain that you have asked him many times and he is still not obeying, and this is acting very irresponsibly. Compare his actions to what you are role modeling. Consider an example where often if you are in the middle of something important, it leads you to being late to pick him up from school. He wants you to be on time. His definition of a timely pick-up is at dismissal time 2:45 p.m., not after dismissal time 3:00 p.m. Consider when you ask him to clear his plate from the table in a timely fashion, and your definition of a timely fashion is right after the meal, what is his definition of a timely fashion to clear his plate? Is it fifteen minutes after you want him to? Is it thirty minutes?

When you hear your child's voice, you are modeling being respectful of his voice. In turn, your child will hear your voice and be respectful to you. This carries out into the world outside his relationship with you. The child whose voice is heard with respect is the child who will hear the voice of his fellow classmates. Your child will not be the kid that grabs the toy out of the other kid's hand. Rather, your child will wait patiently or do something else. Or your child will try to negotiate with words to get the toy he wants. Your younger child will listen when you tell him to stay in front of the house and not run down the street. When your three-year-old is riding his bike and you show him how far it is okay to ride, he will listen. This child will make a responsible choice and be respectful of your voice. It makes him feel good to make a responsible choice because it fits him. It is who he is.

If you want your teenager to leave you a note when he gets home from school (if you are not at home) indicating where he is going and the approximate time he will return, you need to do the same for him. The parent who says, "I am the parent; therefore I don't have to answer to my teen, whereas he has to answer to me," is the parent who will have a disrespectful teen. It is not answering to your teen when you leave a note for him, but rather it is treating him as an equal member of the family. Therefore, it is courteous and respectful to leave him a note if you are going to be late or are going somewhere when he expects you to be home. Whatever the age of the child is, you should have your antennas up as to whether or not you are modeling respectful and responsible behavior for your child, and directed at your child.

As you are making an active shift to role model respectful and responsible behavior, it is helpful to discuss this behavior with your child. If you are wondering if your preschool child is too young to have this discussion, the answer is no. If you are wondering if your teen is too old to have this discussion, the answer is also no. No matter what your child's age is, it is important to openly communicate with him, and explain that you believe it may be possible that there is a connection between your behavior and his. Tell your child that you think it may be possible that he is learning from you, and explain to your child the concept of role modeling and its connection to learned behavior. The parenting a child receives teaches him how to interact with that parent, himself, and others. Ask your child if he agrees with this philosophy, or does he believe that we all exist in a vacuum, and one does not affect the other? If you provide a child the opportunity to analyze and discuss philosophies, he will take the opportunity to explore.

Next, tell your child that, just as you want to act in a respectful and responsible way toward him, you are hopeful that he feels the same way and wants to act respectfully toward you. Explore what you envision a potential positive shift will look like. Discuss concrete examples of behaviors that are applicable to your relationship so your child can understand what real life examples you are referring to. Talk about what you will be doing differently, and ask your child what shifts in behavior he can also make. Ask him what he envisions in a respectful and responsible parent, what he sees and would like to see.

MODELING RESPECTFUL AND RESPONSIBLE BEHAVIOR IN TERMS OF YOUR CHILD'S OBSERVATIONS OF YOU TOWARD OTHERS

Remember the four questions you were instructed to ask yourself when modeling respectful and responsible choices in your interactions with your child? For this next part of Technique #5, role modeling respect, ask yourself the same four questions again, but this time substitute the notion of how you interact *directly* toward your child with how you interact *with others*. For example, you can now ask yourself this version of the first question: "In my opinion, in what ways do I show that I am respectful to others each day?" Consider situations your child may have already observed or is currently observing. Even if you think your child is not paying attention because he is busy playing, or you think he is too young to absorb what is happening, or too old to be interested, know that he is indeed observing you. Children do not exist in a vacuum. What parents do and say to others is witnessed by our children.

Once you have asked yourself all four questions, substituting how you interact directly toward your child with how you interact with others, then go on to the next step. Ask yourself all four questions, continuing with the notion of how you interact with others, and, this time, substitute the words "disrespectful" and "irresponsible."

Here are some examples of situations that your child observes of your behavior towards others:

You and your child are standing in line at the supermarket and the cashier makes an error with a customer that makes you have to wait longer. You are becoming frustrated, and when you finally reach the cashier, you are less than polite. Your child observes your impolite behavior. Perhaps you are cold to her, perhaps you make a negative comment, perhaps you mumble a nasty comment under your breath, but loud enough so both the cashier and your child can hear you, or perhaps you say something rude about the cashier to the person behind you in the line. You are being disrespectful to the cashier, and your child is watching. She has now witnessed you being disrespectful to another person. You figure your child was not really paying attention. Perhaps your child is two and was singing to herself. Perhaps your child is seven and was trying to add some very big numbers in her head. Perhaps your child is a teen and was text messaging a friend. You pay for your groceries and leave the store and forget about this incident, but your child remembers how you modeled disrespectful behavior.

A few weeks later, your child's teacher or day care worker (depending on the age of the child), calls you and reports that your child has been muttering disrespectful comments about her or other children in the class. Do you see any connection between what this child learned from your behavior in the shopping line and what she is doing now? Do you take any responsibility for this? This is an example of the importance of modeling respectful behavior and acting responsibly.

Picture the scenario where a divorced parent named Jennifer states to her child, "I am so angry at your father I am going to make sure he pays for leaving us. I might not be able to hurt him physically, but I am going to hurt him where it hurts; right in his wallet!" Let's not deny the pain this woman is feeling, but it is still important that she is cautious in what she vocalizes. Imagine a scenario where Jennifer's daughter, Lisa, is angry at her sister Jeannie. While Jeannie is asleep, Lisa cuts a big chunk of hair off Jeannie's head. This shows a high level of disrespect and is a very irresponsible choice. When Jennifer talks with her daughter, Lisa responds, "I just got sis where it hurts. She hurt me so bad when she read my diary, so now I hurt her. Her hair is her favorite thing." Do you see the connection between what the divorced mother said and what her daughter did? Being respectful and making responsible choices can be role modeled when you relate to others.

I cannot stress enough the importance of both positive role-modeling and discussing respectful and responsible behavior with your child. No matter what your child's age is, it is important to discuss the improvements you plan to make in regard to how you relate to others. That discussion will help to develop a wonderful relationship as the years go by. In addition, the child feels that you are treating him as an equal member of the family if you are taking the time to explain this philosophical notion to him.

Remember that the Dr. Karen Parenting Philosophy is carried out in the nine techniques. If you keep the philosophy in mind, you will make healthy, helpful choices for you and those you love.

As a fellow human being, I am aware that when it comes to human emotions and actions, we cannot always be as rational as we would like. We do not always act in the best way possible, or consider how our words will affect our children in terms of them becoming respectful and making responsible choices. Just as parents may err at times, we must also recognize that our children make mistakes in judgment too. There may be moments of disrespect and irresponsible choices. If, more often than not, we can do our best to be aware of our own thoughts and actions, if we can do our best to consider what our words and actions signify, then we can do our best to make wise choices to help our children experience us as respectful and responsible parents. They will grow to become adults who are cognizant of their choices. They will become adults who respect themselves and others, and make responsible choices.

In regard to Technique #5, role modeling, allow

yourself to take inventory of your experiences in relating to your children and to others. Use the four questions to successfully implement Technique #5 and view your actions honestly. You will thus learn and grow, and help your children to be respectful and make responsible choices.

CHAPTER 8

TECHNIQUE #6: SAY THANK YOU AND YOU ARE WELCOME

This chapter may be the shortest of all the chapters, but it certainly should not be ignored. Do not be fooled into thinking that just a few pages implies that there is a message of insignificance. Good things not only come in big packages but in small packages as well, just as important points come in big chapters and small. No matter how old your child is, saying "thank you" and "you are welcome" to your child, is a very important part of one's daily interaction.

Saying *thank you* as well as y*ou are welcome* shows your respect for another person. It is expressing that you appreciate what they have done for you, and shows that you value them as a person. Furthermore, when another person has said, "Thank you" to you, when you reply, "You are welcome," this shows that you appreciate they took the time to let you know they appreciate what you have done for them. You must be special to them, an important and valued person. You feel respected.

I recall during my youth that my mother believed that it was important to teach manners through example. Thus, she certainly with consistency would say *thank you* and *you are welcome*. Although in my house during my youth, this communication went beyond just simply teaching good manners. I can remember a funny little thing that my mother used to do that I now call the "thank you, you are welcome dance." As I also incorporated my mother's "dance" into my own life with my son, I have determined that the "thank you, you are welcome dance" is one of the nine techniques for raising children that are respectful and make responsible choices.

Why does Dr. Karen suggest that saying *thank you* and *you are welcome* is a dance? The following is an example to provide the answer to this question. The example is sneezing. I can clearly remember the dance in our home in Queens, New York. My mother would sneeze, I would say, "Bless you," she would say, "Thank you", and I would say, "You are welcome." If it had stopped there, that would have been sufficient. But my mother took the *thank you* and the *you are welcome* further, which is what I believe really made the significant impact in my life. She would continue, "Thank you for saying you are welcome." I would add, "You are welcome for saying thank you for saying you are welcome." She continued, "You are welcome for saying thank you for saying you are welcome for saying thank you." This went back and forth for as long as we wanted to do the dance. You get the idea?

This little dance is emblematic of how good a parent-child relationship can be if we just take the time to appreciate, value, and respect each other. This becomes a relationship where, no matter what one person is in the middle of doing, they stop for a moment just to show that they care about the other person. I remember that when my mother was in another room working on something that I knew was very important for my father, and if I happened to sneeze during that time, I heard her call out, "Bleeeeeeessss youuuuuu." Yes, she would still take the time out for the thank you, you are welcome dance even when she was busy. Did that make Karen the child feel special and valued? Yes it did.

Whether your seven-month-old takes your shoe out of the rack and hands it to you, or your one-year-old picks up his sock instead of leaving it in the middle of the floor, or your five-year-old helps you push the garbage pail to the curb on garbage day, or your ten-year-old hands you the pepper at the dinner table before you even ask because he knows you like pepper on your mashed potatoes, or your sixteen-year-old carries his candy bar wrapper to the garbage after having a snack in the family room, or your children notice you saying thank you to your spouse for making dinner or changing a light bulb, or stopping for milk on the way home from work; no matter what the "little stuff" is, it shows that members of your family respect and appreciate each other when you say thank you and you are welcome.

A parent can use this dance to role model respect. As we have discussed, a child who feels respected is a child who feels valued for who he is, and wants to act in a responsible way. If you incorporate Technique #6 into your family, it can help make a difference both within your family and outside it.

CHAPTER 9

TECHNIQUE #7: CREATE A SENSE OF ORDER IN THE WORLD

Creating a sense of order in the world for the purposes of this book means creating a sense of order in your home, for your home is your child's world. When there is order in a child's home, he can develop expectations of what *feels right* in terms of mutual respectful and responsible behavior. When things are not "right," he has a core understanding of what is right, a baseline and a ground upon which to build choices in terms of how to deal and cope with something that is not right.

It is therefore important to have order in your home. When I use the term order, I mean providing children with a sense of emotional and physical safety and stability, plus providing these things in a respectful environment. From my clinical perspective, creating order at home includes providing an experience for your child where there are (1) *boundaries* and (2) *routine and structure*. This is important if you want to raise children that are respectful of self and others.

BOUNDARIES

ENVIRONMENT

From an environmental perspective, setting boundaries means that you are respectful of the other person's belongings and privacy. When you respect your child's environment, you knock before you enter your child's room. Whether you have a young child or a teenager, children need to feel you are respecting their boundaries if you expect them to act respectfully. For an example, it is important to ask before you take apart a train track construction on the floor so you can vacuum. You let your child play a role in deciding how to decorate his room, e.g., what posters he wants on the wall. You model respect of another's environment.

Being respectful of your child's environment is teaching your child what healthy and appropriate boundaries are. Your child will carry these lessons along with him when he relates to family members, friends, and others. For example, if you are respectful of your child's environmental boundaries, when you have a stack of paper for work on your desk at home, your child will not just take a piece of paper out of your pile and write on it. He will be respectful of your stuff (your environment) because you are respectful of his stuff (his environment). Another example is when your child goes to his grandparents' house, he will take off his sneakers before entering (if that is their house rule), he will not pull the little glass and ceramic figures off of the shelf (yes, even as young as two years old) because he has learned to be respectful of another person's environment. And still another example is that your teen will ask before using the telephone at his cousin's or friend's house. He will ask if it is okay if he turns on the radio station he likes at his aunt's house rather than just walking over to the radio and turning on what he wants with no consideration of others.

Give children of any age the opportunity to experience boundaries. This will help them develop boundary-appropriate behavior, and understand boundaries that others have. What feels right thus leads to healthy, respectful, and responsible behaviors. You will find that your child will tend to gravitate toward making friends with those that hold a similar value system. Your child will not be the one to knock down another child's blocks, nor will he laugh when a child knocks down another kid's blocks. Your twelve-year-old will not be the one who takes a dare and pulls the fire alarm in school. He will be respectful of the school's environment. If you and your teenager have lost the respectful and responsible behavioral interaction between each other that you had when he was younger, it can absolutely be helped. If you and your teenager never had a respectful relationship between each other, that can be improved. If your teenager is the child that would pull the fire alarm, and he has a pattern of making poor choices, it is not too late to help him help himself to develop better behavioral patterns, including respectful and responsible choices. Discuss with your child the significance of boundaries from an environmental perspective. Discuss with your child how he feels you can improve in your boundary relationship, and ask him in what ways he also can improve.

RELATIONAL/PERSONAL PERSPECTIVE

From a relational/personal perspective, setting boundaries means that you are respectful of the other person's physical space. For example, you tell your infant you are going to change his diaper and say what you are doing while you are doing it, rather than just stripping his clothes off of him and rushing through the diaper change, as if his body is just a table you are cleaning. His body is to be treated kindly. Another example, you ask your two-year-old if it is okay if you zip up his jacket, or does he want to do it? When you do not ask, it is as if you own his body. When you do ask, you are being respectful of your toddler's physical space because this is his body, not yours. Therefore, he will feel respected. This helps to develop a child that develops an instinct to treat his own body (and the bodies of others) respectfully. This is a child who learns healthy boundary relations.

Imagine a scenario where your very young child is acting inappropriately in a public place. You decide that you need to take him outside to cool down. You tell him you are going to pick him up, hold him, and carry him out so that you and he can cool down, after which you will both return. This verbalization to your child, rather than just grabbing him and scooping him up, makes all the difference in terms of whether you are respecting his personal boundaries or not.

If your method is typically to grab your child or relate to him in some other physical way, it may be hard at first to make this very powerful shift. Words are very powerful and much healthier than invading anyone's boundaries. Using words helps your child learn this key lesson. If this is a new pattern your child experiences in terms of how you relate to him, he will see respect in your actions. Chances are that this child will decrease the freaking out and begin acting in a respectful manner.

With most children, if you use words with consistency and your child experiences your respectful interaction, you will not feel the need to have a physical intervention and carry your child out of the room; you will have other options. In addition, you will find that your respect of his personal boundaries, your new style of interaction with him when he is upset (e.g. he is disappointed he did not get a toy in the store he wanted), will have a positive effect on his behavior.

Here is another example: Imagine your teenage girl wearing an outfit that is much more revealing than you feel is appropriate. To put it mildly, you felt like you were going to fall off of your chair when you saw her. If you speak to her instead of grabbing her and pulling at the shirt and skirt to cover her up, this interaction is positive. State your dismay in words, verbalize your concern that her outfit is too revealing in your opinion, and be respectful of your teen's physical boundaries. Discuss your daughter's opinions with her.

Role modeling boundaries in terms of how you relate to your child's physical space not only teaches a child how to relate to himself and others, it also develops a sense of right and wrong in the child. For example, if you feel it is okay to hit your child when you are angry, your child learns that the way to deal with anger is with a physical reaction. The child also learns that it feels right when you are angry to respond physically. The child becomes used to it. A child who experiences parents who respect his physical space and knows that there are physical boundaries is a child who, if another child or an adult touches him inappropriately, will discern the inappropriateness.

The choices parents make affect their children both in the short-term and in the long-term. Think about other examples. Here is a long-term example. Consider the mate a boy named Jonathan chooses in his future. If as a child, Jonathan experienced a sense of order in his world, in terms of boundaries, he will pick a mate who is respectful of him as a person, and is respectful of herself. These healthy adults will feel good as individuals and raise children that learn respectful, healthy, responsible boundaries.

The next element of Technique #7, creating a sense of order in your child's world, is giving your child routine and structure.

ROUTINE AND STRUCTURE

When a child has *rules* to live by in the home environment, he has a sense of and a belief in order. He develops a feeling that *routine* and *structure* feel good. Therefore, when this child is outside his own home, he is respectful of the rules of others. In addition, a child who knows what to expect through the use of routine and structure experiences a sense of calm, safety, and security because he knows he can rely on his routine.

Although routine and structure are important, it is also important to note that the home is not the military. There also needs to be a comfortable amount of flexibility at home. To be so structured that there is no room for flexibility, or to be the opposite, where things are so laid-back that there is no routine and structure, is not helpful in teaching a child to be respectful and make responsible choices.

For example, the child who sees a sense of routine and structure along with flexibility in his home is the child who successfully integrates with other children in school and gets along. He is liked by other children and seen in a positive way by the teachers. One may ask, "Why is this?" The answer is that the child who learns to expect routine and structure at home also expects it at school and elsewhere. When your child experiences routine and structure at home, along with some flexibility, he will follow the rules and routines at school responsibly. When something changes, he will also be able to cope with change. It is these behaviors that are pleasant qualities for others to be around.

In your home, an example of routine and structure might be your typical morning scenario. Your child wakes up, says good morning to you, uses the bathroom, brushes his teeth, gets dressed, eats breakfast, watches television, and goes to school. As explained above, flexibility within this structure is important. For example, there may be some days when your child wakes up hungry and would like to eat breakfast before he gets dressed. To insist that the morning routine cannot be altered is going overboard and does not teach respectful and responsible behavior. It is important that you are supportive of his awareness of what his body needs, and hear his voice. But if his voice says, "Television first," and you want to teach him that responsibilities come first on a school day, it is best to preserve the regular structure. Your child can thus learn what his responsibilities are, and that sometimes he can change the order (e.g., eat first), as long as he takes care of his responsibilities (e.g., gets dressed before watching television). This helps him develop a sense of confidence. He also learns that you feel you can rely on him to make responsible choices.

Children learn to relate in a respectful manner to themselves, other people, and their belongings. They act responsibly in their interactions because it "fits" and feels right, not out of fear. Being respectful and making responsible choices out of fear and/or just because your parent said to do it has short-lived results. Eventually, children grow up and become independent. The idea is to help your child become an independent individual who is respectful and makes responsible choices because *that is who he is.* Boundaries, routine, and structure lead to positive development of your children as you implement Technique #7 and create a sense of order in your children's world.

CHAPTER 10

TECHNIQUE #8: SPEND QUALITY TIME: THREE KINDS

This chapter focuses on the importance of spending quality time with your children. There are three kinds of quality time that will be addressed. Each type is important in its own right, but it is this author's contention that all three are actively needed if one truly wants the results of a respectful and responsible child.

TYPE #1: QUALITY TIME: LET YOUR CHILD HELP YOU

It is very important that children of all ages feel that they can play an active part in your life in terms of helping you. Offering them opportunities to help you is important, even if they do not always take you up on it. Yes, sometimes having your children help you is their choice to make, whereas other times, you ask for the help when you feel your child really needs to help you. Utilizing times when your child helps you as opportunities for one type of quality time holds its own importance.

For example, if you let your five-year-old help you, as a choice, to put the wet clothes into the dryer and take the dry clothes out, this child will be more likely through the years to not only help with the laundry, but to do other household tasks as well. He will be respectful and responsible when you ask him to help you. He will also develop an appreciation for housework and feel that he is an important part of the family. This feeling of value is significantly impacted by his experience of having responsibilities in the house, especially when you express your appreciation for his help, which makes him feel that he is capable and responsible. A child who feels that he is considered as responsible will see himself as responsible. This child will feel that making responsible choices fits him, and he will make responsible choices in and outside the home. Spending time together as a team to complete the task at hand is actually one type of quality time.

If, for example, you are painting the bathroom or fixing the pipe under the sink, let your child help you. Sure, it may take you a bit longer to complete the task, but when a young child learns to help, he will be more likely to help when he gets older. Whether you have a young child or an older child that is helping you, the child learns that you value his help, and he is thus a very important part of the family. This does not mean that your older child should be expected to become a servant. I believe in helping as a choice. But a child who helps develops a sense of ownership of the house. There are times when a child must do something simply because you ask him. Letting your child help you and requesting help includes a fine balance of (a) letting him help you when he requests, (b) asking him to help you but he gets to choose to accept this invitation or not, and (c) making it obvious in a clear and respectful way that help is required.

A child who has the feeling of taking ownership of his home is a child who is allowed to help, but he does not substitute for the parents in terms of household chores. The parents are mainly responsible for the household chores, and the child is still the child. Remember, treating your child as an equal member of the family (see Chapter 2) does not mean the child is required to do everything the parents do. The child who participates in household chores in a healthy, balanced way will learn to respect his environment (his home) and act responsibly (by taking care of tasks), and thus relate to you, his own self, others, and their environments respectfully and responsibly.

The child who gets to help out will always remember the role he played in terms of his household responsibilities. Think about this, and ask yourself what you were responsible for in your home when you were young. Did you feel a sense of ownership in your home? Ask your spouse and your friends about their memories. You will find that most people remember their household jobs, and whether or not they had a sense of ownership of their home.

When your child helps you, there is wonderful quality time to be had. Quality conversation can take place while you and your child are working together on a household task. The quality time makes the child feel special and important.

The following is an example from this clinician's personal life: Shortly after my son turned seven, and we were spending time with my parents, he was trying to help his grandfather with something in the house that needed to be fixed. When my father asked my son how he could know so much about fixing things at such a young age, my son told him, "Daddy taught me everything I know about fixing things." This is a fine example that at a young age, a child recognizes who he is spending time with and learning from. Whenever my husband fixes things around the house, he involves our son. Not only is our son learning how to fix things and taking ownership of his home, but he is also being responsible for taking good care of it, learning how to respectfully work with another person, and feeling good about himself and his capabilities. And he also gets a great deal of quality time with his dad.

TYPE #2: QUALITY TIME: PLAY WITH YOUR CHILD EACH DAY

It is very important that your child plays with you each day. Of course, we all have very busy schedules, and sometimes playtime may be so short that you feel it is not even worth it, but this is not the case. Even ten minutes of quality play with your child is special. There are two types of play. First, there are your child's ideas for play. Second, there are your ideas for play. There will be days you will do your child's ideas of play, and other days when you do your ideas of play, and yet other days when both your child's and your ideas concur. Try to pay attention and find out if you typically focus on only one type of play and rarely include the other. Both kinds are important.

YOUR CHILD'S IDEAS FOR PLAY

Choosing to do what your child wants to do, your child's ideas, makes him feel that his ideas are good. That helps him to feel good about himself and confident in his own ideas. His self-confidence affects how he relates to other children. He feels special when you play with him, and sees that he is valued because you are expressing interest in his ideas. If he feels valued, he feels respected. A child who feels valued and respected is a child who acts in a respectful way to others. This child will make wise choices. This child will develop confidence to listen to his own inner voice and come up with good ideas because he learned from you that you feel his ideas are worthy of being heard.

YOUR IDEAS FOR PLAY

Coming up with ideas for playing with your child is also important. When a child feels that his parent is taking the time out to come up with special ideas to play with him, it plays a role in his feeling special. A person who feels special also feels good about himself. He will treat others kindly. The ideas you come up with can be of your own creation or ideas you find in books or magazines. Your idea is your suggestion.

You can and must incorporate this notion of including your child's ideas for play as well as your own for children of all ages. Certainly the age of your child may impact how often you are actually playing. For an example, the older child may have more commitments than the younger child. Therefore, parent-child play may be based on your older child's schedule. Do not let time pass and get so busy that an entire week goes by and you and your teen have not interacted in a playful manner. When I say make time for play every day, perhaps for the teen, play may be a car ride somewhere. Use that car ride as an opportunity to chat about something that is meaningful in your teen's life. If you do not know your teen's interests, then this is the time to find out. Ask your teenager what his interests are.

Sometimes talk is play. For example, if you have a conversation about clothes with your teen, this is a kind of play. Perhaps you take a look at one of the fashion magazines your preteen and/or teen is reading and ask what she thinks of the outfit that so-and-so wore. "So-and-so" is, of course, today's popular celebrity. If you do not know, get in the know. Being an informed parent is imperative. For the teen that is very into video games, take time while he is playing to stop what you are doing to check it out, and perhaps even try one round with him. If you enjoy playing tennis and your teen is into baseball, you can ask your teen if his strength in baseball could perhaps apply to your tennis swing, as you would like to improve it. This discussion can lead to a discussion where your teen informs you it is a very different kind of swing. You might ask if he would like to try tennis with you, or perhaps you can go to the batting cages with your teen. Quality time is always important.

Quite often, I hear parents report that when their child was younger, they could figure out how to play, how to interact with their child, but now that their child is a preteen or a teen, the old connection is lost. There is no more playing and that is a shame. To play with your teen just needs you to be on a teen's level. It is this clinician's hope that you will make it a point to find play in what you and your children are interested in, and you will take and make the time to discover and spend quality time together.

TYPE #3: QUALITY TIME: ATTENDING TO ERRANDS AND TAKING CARE OF RESPONSIBILITIES

Running errands is a wonderful opportunity to incorporate quality time. For the younger child, on the car ride on the way to an errand, you can ask what games he wants to play, like seeing how many colors you can each spot, taking turns to say what color you see. You can also play the alphabet game where you take turns looking for something that begins with each letter of the alphabet, from A to Z, before you reach your destination. You may need to teach your child these games, so they would at first fall into the category of your ideas for play. Later, your child may express interest in playing one of your games, making it his idea to choose what to play. With the older child, you may try to stump each other with math problems. With the even older child who is almost ready to take driving lessons, you can talk about road signs and what they mean, so he will ace the driving exam. You can test each other by asking, for example, what does the double yellow line represent?

While in the car on the way to do an errand, you can ask your child if he thinks it is time to fill the gas tank. Talk about how people have different philosophies of filling up. Some wait till the tank is half empty, whereas others wait till it is almost on empty. This discussion is for children of all ages. Car talks can be especially interesting to teens. You can also ask your teen his opinion about car care.

In the supermarket, even your young child can help you find what you are looking for. As your young child gets a bit older, he can push the shopping cart, which is a big responsibility. The age of your child determines the kind of help you can request, of course. If your child is learning to read, he can help you read the signs. If he is a teenager, you can consider splitting the shopping list and then meeting at the checkout stand when both lists have been completed. You can even be silly about it and have a race to see who finishes first.

In summary of this chapter on spending quality time with your children, you, the reader, have learned three types of quality time. This quality time helps your child feel that he is a valued and equal member of the family. At any age, he will learn that he is not insignificant but important, necessary, and a valued member of the family team.

CHAPTER 11

TECHNIQUE #9: DO NOT PUSH A PULL DOOR

A technique that has worked before or typically works, but suddenly is not working anymore leads many parents to feel at a loss as to what to do. Parents find themselves still trying to incorporate the same, familiar technique, the same solution that has worked before, and they continue to try to make it work. Parents often tell themselves, "If I keep doing what I am doing, it's bound to work." The fact is that if a technique is no longer working, even though it makes no sense to you why it would not be working anymore, if you continue to try using it, you are repeating the same mistake. You are pushing a pull door. As we all know, no matter how hard you try, you simply cannot open a pull door by pushing it. You can use Technique #9 to figure out why the old technique no longer works, and then develop and utilize a different one.

In other cases, rather than it being a technique that usually works and no longer is working, parents report, "I have tried everything and nothing works." The "everything" parents refer to is actually implementing more of the same, but on the surface it looks different. In essence, the parents feel like they are trying different ideas even though it is the same idea.

If your idea is not working, you can resolve the problem at hand by reviewing the techniques offered in this book, and determining which category your idea falls under. Then pick a different technique. Remember, a round peg does not and cannot fit in a square hole.

A trick I can teach you to help you to pick the "right technique" at the right time so that you can stop pushing a pull door is to ask yourself the following questions:

Question #1: Am I treating my child as a valued member within and of the family?

Question #2: What is my child's voice saying that I might be missing/not hearing?

Question #3: How does his behavior make sense in context?

Technique #9, stop pushing a pull door, is to take the time to consider all of the techniques stated in this book. If you ask yourself three questions, your answers will help you determine what your answer is to incorporate the new technique. If you ask yourself these three questions, your answers will break down the problem and help you generate a solution. It is hard to stop pushing a pull door because we often remain stuck in our belief system of what *should* be working. Here is my suggestion in bottom-line form: stop focusing your energy on the notion of what *should* be working; instead, ask yourself the three questions. They will lead you to figure out that the solution is to pull the pull door. You will figure out what the pull door is.

Technique #9, stop pushing a pull door, is actually a technique to review all of the techniques given in the Dr. Karen Parenting Philosophy. Then consider which technique to incorporate.

For example, consider the scenario where a teenager has been informed by her doctor that she has an illness that may require surgery. Each time her mother asks her questions to monitor her ailments, as per the doctor's orders, the daughter answers the questions in a rude manner. She is downright disrespectful to her mother. Other times, the daughter does not even answer the mother's questions and verbalizes that she wants her mother to stop bothering her. The mother and daughter typically have a good communicative relationship. Their interaction has not been as positive as it usually is since the family has become aware that the daughter may need surgery. The mother-daughter communication pattern of directness has typically been a style that works for their relationship. Thus, the mother continues to try to get the answer from her daughter by asking her the same question about her ailments several times throughout the day. The daughter becomes progressively more and more irritated. The mother feels awful that the typical communication style that she uses with her daughter, direct questions, is not working and thus she is at a loss as to what to do.

In this case, the mother asks Dr. Karen what she can do differently as a parent to be more effective. The mother wants to know what her daughter's ailments are, specifically whether they are occurring and when. The clinician provides this concerned and loving mother with the above three questions to ask herself. It is in that moment, when the mother asks herself the questions documented above, that she recognizes that perhaps her daughter's voice is saying that she is scared. It is not that the teenager does not want to confide in her mother, or that she wants to be rude or disrespectful. It is not that the relationship between them is growing apart. It is not that the daughter is being irresponsible about her illness. Rather, she is closing the door to her mother's questions so as to not answer them, by pushing her mother away. The daughter is doing this because she herself is concerned. To answer her mother's questions means to confront her own fears and concerns that she may need surgery.

Once the mother understands how her daughter's behavior makes sense in context, she is able to change her style of communicating. The mother now understands that by her daughter shutting down/closing her out from asking questions by being rude, it allows her to not have to consider the answers to the questions. Therefore, as stated above, she does not have to confront her own fear of surgery.

Rather than the mother questioning her daughter about what the ailments are and when they are occurring, which makes the daughter feel like her mother is drilling her and contributes to her already existing fear, the mother has another option. Specifically, the mother can validate her daughter's voice by saying to her that she must be feeling scared. The mother can further communicate with her daughter by asking her if answering her questions of if, what, and when the ailments are occurring, makes her daughter worry that surgery will be necessary.

In this case example, once the teenager felt her voice was heard, in contrast to the old technique of being asked to provide her mother with a report, the daughter's seemingly disrespectful and irresponsible behavior ceased to exist because it no longer made sense in context, as the context was taken away. This is an example where the mother was no longer pushing a pull door. She just needed to figure out that she was pushing a pull door and what technique to use. In this case, pulling the door was utilizing Technique #1, Hear the Voice of Your Child and Technique #2, Understand That All Behavior Makes Sense in Context. Take Away the Context. Pushing the door was utilizing direct questions, which was the mother's old style.

The following provides the reader with two examples where a parent thinks she is trying different methods, but it is actually more of the same. The first example is about a mother named Anna and her thirteen-year-old son, Sean. Anna states, "My son won't carry his laundry basket to the laundry room no matter how many different ways I ask him, and I have asked him every way possible. I have tried nicely, calmly, forcefully, angrily. I have been very patient and now I have lost my patience because I have tried everything." Anna feels Sean is being irresponsible because he is not taking care of his chore. She also feels he is being disrespectful because he is not obeying her request.

The example of Anna and Sean is an example of pushing a pull door. Although Anna feels she has tried everything, the fact is that she is trying the same thing over and over again with a different tone. The theme remains the same. Utilizing a different tone inflection is not enough of an actual difference to be considered a difference. If you are pushing a pull door while hopping on one foot, or pushing a pull door while standing with both feet flat, you are still pushing a pull door. The same is true of the above example.

An example of something different that this mother

could do is to look at Dr. Karen's techniques and pick the one where she hears her thirteen-year-old son's voice. His voice is stating that it is not a good time right now to carry down the laundry basket. His voice states that he is too busy to carry it down. In essence, his voice is communicating that there is never a good time for him to do this chore. Without Sean actually stating these words, Anna can certainly recognize this is his voice if she considers his actions. His consistent actions are that he does not take down the basket.

Once Anna heard her son's voice, she would then interact with him differently. If there is never a good time, in his opinion, then any way she asks will not lead to a successful outcome. Rather, the mother could ask Sean if he could help her to develop a plan for when he could slot in a time to bring down the laundry basket. She can further explain that she understands he is a teenager and therefore a busy fellow, and thus there never really is a convenient time. Anna could take it a step further and communicate to her son that she understands the laundry is not his priority as he has many other things going on in his life, but that she does know that having clean clothes matters to him.

The second example to drive home the point that there are times when a parent believes she is trying a different method to change her child's irresponsible or disrespectful behavior, but in fact her method is more of the same, is as follows:

An eight-year-old girl named Tali becomes argumentative when her father, Heath, tells her it is time to turn off the television. Heath reports that Tali becomes nasty and quite disrespectful. Heath reports that there is always a request from Tali for one more show. If he lets her have one more, there is then a request for one more. Heath reports that she seems to want to be in charge and she is not the parent, he is. The father expresses that he feels he has tried everything except throwing the television in the garbage. He reports that he has asked nicely, he tried saying that if she does not turn it off, then he will, he has asked with a stern voice, he has tried giving her a five-minute reminder, and he tried consequences if she does not listen.

Utilizing the Dr. Karen Parenting Philosophy, the parent needs to figure out what he can do that is different. All of Heath's attempts are under the heading of the same theme: the theme of him telling her what to do. Therefore, the daughter does not feel in control, rather her father is in charge. He is telling her when to turn off the television. Just like the example of Anna and Sean, a different tone inflection, or a different way of wording the request does not make the method different. One might think adding consequences appears to be different, but it is more of the theme of he is telling her what to do, and proving he is in charge by creating consequences.

Considering the Dr. Karen techniques, which might be the one to consider? Remember the three questions addressed in this chapter to help figure out which technique to use? Look back at those questions and consider this scenario. The scenario of Tali and Heath is a great candidate for utilizing the technique; "all behaviors make sense in context". In this case, the context is a power-struggle between father and daughter. If the power struggle is taken away, then the context will cease to exist, and therefore the problem behavior (argumentative, disrespectful) will cease to exist.

The father had it right when he reported that her behavior seems to be that she wants to be in charge. When he tells her what to do, she feels like he is trying to be in control and therefore her power is taken away. In this case, after exploring the creative options, as creativity for parents is important, the plan was that he would purchase an egg timer with her at the store. They jointly decided that first she could set the timer to a choice of 30 minutes or 60 minutes, up to her, and then the timer would let her know when her choice of time was up, and then it would be time for her to turn off the television.

CHAPTER 12

THE CHALLENGES YOU MAY FACE WHEN LIVING BY THE DR. KAREN PARENTING PHILOSOPHY

As you know now that you have read this book, the Dr. Karen Parenting Philosophy is to treat your child as an equal member of the family. This means that your child's voice is important and he is a valued voice of the family team. This philosophy and the nine techniques educates the reader on how to raise respectful and responsible children. If your child has a voice in the family and you truly hear it, as recommended in Technique #1, you will absolutely get to know your child. If you know your child, then you can make choices that help him meet his potential and feel good about himself as an individual. He in turn then grows up to be an adult who knows himself and has the core value system that will help him be respectful and make responsible choices. He can see himself in a positive light.

There will be times that holding the Dr. Karen Parenting Philosophy will lead to challenges. Just as Dr. Karen has encountered challenges, be aware that you will also experience challenges. I am cheering for you that you do not allow challenges to prevent you from raising respectful children who make responsible choices. Sometimes, challenges can steer us away from doing something we know we want to do as well as believe we should. An expression that many of us are familiar with is that people are their own worst enemy. Oh yes, that is true. We often know something is good for us, and yet it is a challenge to do that something so we choose not to do what is good for us. Then there are times we think we know what is good for us, but someone has a different opinion, and we find ourselves questioning our original opinion. There will be times when others raise their eyebrow at your parenting choices. This can lead to even the biggest fans of the Dr. Karen Parenting Philosophy questioning what they are doing, and seeking out validation.

Yes, if implemented, this very philosophy you have just read about may lead to you experiencing challenges. Consider these two key statements:

1. We do not do what we know is good for us because it is usually hard work and thus challenging.

2. When others have opinions that differ from ours, sometimes we are influenced by those opinions. We may even question our original opinion.

To my dear readers, know this:

1. Facing the challenges you may experience in living the Dr. Karen Parenting Philosophy is worth it. Doing the work is worth it because you and your family are worth it.

2. Try your best not to give in to negative peer pressure to parent differently if this is the philosophy you hold dear. Do what you know is right for you and your family. Each day, you have to answer to yourself and your family, not to those outside of it. You want to be able to look in the mirror and feel proud of the choices you make to help your child

be a respectful and responsible person.

You may wonder: Why in the world did this author write about challenges the reader may encounter? Wouldn't the author want to paint only a rosy picture? The answer is that I want you to know the challenges you may face so that when you do, you can recognize them. You can be prepared to face the challenges rather than being drowned by them. With this awareness, you will understand that a challenge is just an obstacle on your journey. You can go over it, under it, through it, or around it. Listen to your inner voice. If this philosophy works for you, then who should you let influence you otherwise? Challenges are not barriers that you will allow to prevent you from reaching your goals. Challenges are normal and natural parts of everyday life; allowing you to think about the choices you are making, and to confirm and validate that you are making choices that work for you and your family.

The first challenge to know is that it is *work* to incorporate my philosophy. No one can do it for you. You need to take the time to be aware of your interactions with your children. Each day, there will be opportunities both small and large that will allow you to either incorporate the Dr. Karen Parenting Philosophy or not. Although it is work that has paid off for many families, just the fact that it is *work* on your part is a challenge. If you are up for the challenge, how joyous you will find those moments when you see that your parenting philosophy is indeed paying off.

The notion that what you put in is what you get out is a lovely notion, in theory. It is exciting to see it come true. When you put into your children the teachings of respectful and responsible behavior, and you see them behaving in that way, you have a special feeling. Once you do the work, with consistency and practice, it will become a more natural style of interacting with your children. Once you incorporate the Dr. Karen Parenting Philosophy and see how it works successfully, you will be motivated to continue, and it will not be work anymore. It will be a way of life that makes as much sense as peeing in the toilet rather than on the floor of your home. (Was that disgusting? It drove the point home though!)

Now that I have forewarned you that one of the challenges is that it is work to apply the Dr. Karen Parenting Philosophy, let's move on to the next challenge that you may face. The second challenge is that there will be people that will disagree with this philosophy.

Holding this philosophy as your own and incorporating it in your life comes with a warning label: "Others will disagree with this philosophy."

You may wonder why others will disagree with this philosophy, and how that may be a problem for you. It may be a problem for you because often, when others disagree, they will interact with you in a way that can be quite rude. That can be uncomfortable. Often, when people feel strongly about how they live, in essence, people do have a general philosophy on child rearing, even if they do not outwardly explain it. If they are then faced with the Dr. Karen Parenting Philosophy, they become defensive about their own philosophy.

Often, those with a different philosophy feel that their philosophy of child rearing is being questioned when they encounter a different one from theirs, and then they become argumentative. Just as the writer of this book does not tell others they are wrong for their parenting style if it is different from the Dr. Karen Parenting Philosophy, you should not feel you are required to do so either. You can go so far as to tell the other person that this is the style that feels right for you, and say you are not questioning what they are doing. In essence, everyone is entitled to their own opinion. Even with this statement, you will often discover that those with a different parenting philosophy will feel threatened, as though their entire person is being put on the evaluation block.

When someone attends this clinician's workshop, then he is open-minded enough to hear the philosophy and the techniques. In addition, it is that person that typically incorporates what was discussed with success, even if he came in questioning the philosophy. When parents come to this clinician's office looking for guidance, they are usually sincere about their desire to make a shift. They are willing to try out the Dr. Karen Parenting Philosophy because everything else they have done to this point has failed.

If you are reading this book, perhaps you are also in a place in your life where you are interested in learning a new philosophy that focuses on raising respectful children who make responsible choices. There will be many times when you will encounter someone who you cannot sit down and have a philosophical discussion with, and educate them on the philosophy or the nine techniques. I know this, not just based on what my clients and workshop attendees report, but from my own first-hand experiences through the years.

When you incorporate the Dr. Karen Philosophy into your life, others may observe and notice how well it works.

They may become curious and want to learn more.

This chapter draws upon this clinician's examples from personal experiences. Some clinicians that also are writers may question this entire chapter. A clinician divulging the personal challenges she faced when incorporating the very philosophy being taught in this book, may seem different from the typical style of writing. To the other clinicians that are excited about my candor, I smile and say it is my pleasure. To you, my readers, it is this clinician's intent to include personal examples of the struggles I experienced to help you to stay true to this philosophy when you are also challenged.

Perhaps my challenges will provide you with the reassurance and acknowledgement that you are not alone on this parenting journey. If the one and only Dr. Karen faced judgment, critique, and opposing views, and can acknowledge its challenge, then you, as a reader, can be patient and kind to yourself during your journey. You can remain true to this philosophy and its techniques even when there are some that disagree. You can choose to consistently continue to implement the methodology you so desire to follow because of what it provides to you and your family, because you know it is what you so desire. Live your life for you and those you love, not for those that are the externals in your life. You are going into this parenting style not disillusioned that it is an easy road.

The real life examples in this chapter are often focused with regard to the use of Technique #1, Hear the Voice of Your Child. Technique #1 drives the Dr. Karen Parenting Philosophy. It is the technique that is woven throughout all the other techniques that make this philosophy go from theory to action. Therefore, it is the technique that most often rubs others the wrong way.

THE CRYING INFANT EPISODE

When my son was an infant, he cried during the night. This is typical behavior in infants. My approach was to go in, hug him, and talk to him until he felt at peace and fell asleep again. That was what felt right to me, to hear my son's voice. It was my opinion that his infant voice was expressing a desire for nurturing. I therefore heard his voice and nurtured him. During that time in my life, I was interested in what the popular books were saying about the nighttime waking of infants. Most of the popular books focused on the importance of helping your infant to develop independence and self-reliance by teaching him to "self-soothe," by not replying to his request for loving affection.

During that time in my son's development, and my own growth as a parent, reading those types of books was mentally challenging. When you believe something different from what many of the books you find on promoting a particular philosophy, you feel you are in the minority.

When a person feels she is in the minority, she cannot help but to analyze and re-evaluate her own thoughts and decisions. Often, a person at that point questions whether there is a possibility that she is wrong, even when she feels what she is doing is right. It is this clinician's belief that questioning yourself is healthy. It is important to self-introspect and consider all possibilities. It is our questions, our evaluating and re-evaluating our philosophies during different times in our life that helps us to grow and enhance our lives. With that being said, staying true to the Dr. Karen Parenting Philosophy was important to me as a parent. It is this philosophy that has become clearer every day of my personal and professional life. In my personal life, what actually helped me all those years ago was that my husband's philosophy was (and still is) in sync with mine. As a parent, it helps to have your spouse supportive of your parenting style. This is not the case for all marriages. I have couples that attend counseling for help with how to work through that very issue, but that is not the focus of this chapter. Perhaps this writer can consider a book in the future on how to parent when parents have different philosophies.

It is the opinion of this clinician that for a child to truly learn to self-soothe, he must first learn that he can rely on his parent to be there for him. Not coming to your child's nighttime call teaches him that it is wrong to request nurturing from his parents. This is not a healthy message, and the child will learn that his voice does not matter. In contrast, when an infant learns that you will come to his aid when he calls, he also learns that he is worthy of being soothed. Therefore, he treats himself more kindly as he grows up. He learns through example when you model soothing techniques by going into his room when he cries during the night, then giving him a hug and telling him he is loved. This will turn into self-soothing as he learns to do these things for himself through your role modeling, and through your interactions with him as he ages. He will thus be able to self-soothe in a healthy, positive, self-healing way.

As a family therapist, I suggest that an infant that was nurtured (e.g., his nighttime voice was heard) becomes a teenager who will also seek out healthy ways to soothe himself when he experiences stressful situations in school. The soothing could take the form of talking to you, playing sports with his friends, reading a book, listening to music, or writing in a journal, instead of pushing his feelings away because no one has ever been interested in hearing his voice. If no one has ever heard his voice, as the years go onward, this child may turn to unhealthy methods of coping, such as avoiding his feelings. For an example, pushing down one's feelings with overeating, trying to escape from or not attending to his feelings by drinking alcohol, or doing drugs are unhealthy methods that truly do not attend to his feelings. Rather, these methods are unhealthy means of not coping.

Your infant can learn that he can count on those he loves to be there for him. Then he will learn to communicate his feelings (healthy life skill) rather than push his feelings aside and keep them inside (unhealthy life skill). As he grows older, he will be there for others when they need him. Along with positive self-soothing, he will learn true compassion for others. He will treat others respectfully because he was treated respectfully by you.

When we do not help to soothe a crying infant, that infant learns that he must just deal with not being heard, that others will not help him. He will not learn empathy or compassion. He learns it is each man for himself. He is learning that he has no choice but to just deal with wanting to feel a connection with another person, and that his needs are not worth much. He learns to suck it up because no one is going to hug him even if he begs.

I shall take this line of thinking a step further into the future and suggest that when this infant becomes an adult, he is a candidate for not being compassionate to his spouse in a verbal nor action oriented way. For an example, consider the following case scenario: The wife says to her husband, "Honey, I am feeling very lonely. I miss you when you go out with your friends every weekend. Three nights out of the week, you work late, another two you are at the bar, and the final two, you are so tired that you just go in your room. Your kids miss you. Let's spend more time together and go on a date together. Let's do more things as a family." He replies, "Stop trying to control me. I work all week, and I deserve to do what I want." This is a man who thinks being responsible and respectful to his children and wife is nothing more than bringing home a paycheck, and has nothing to do with affection, attention, and time. This is being disrespectful to his wife, not even considering her feelings or her solution as an option. She is looking to him for a relationship, but he is pushing her out of his life, not soothing her. This is the same man who wonders why his wife says she wants a divorce when the children are older.

In the above example, I fast-forwarded to what an un-soothed child can potentially grow up to become. I hope I made my point. Although just because a parent did not incorporate my philosophy of child rearing when their child was an infant, this does not mean the child is messed up for life. There are daily opportunities for parents of children of all ages to make a positive difference in their child's life. It also does not mean a guarantee of the above scenario of the disconnected husband. I wanted to make the point that the choices you make today do and will affect your child today or tomorrow. The fast forward example could occur. The authors who promote self-soothing feel they are right. In my experience working with families since 1993, I have seen that if you treat your child as an equal and valued member of the family, and thus hear your child's voice, your child will grow up to be a respectful and responsible adult.

As you can see, this author can spend time countering the opinions of the authors of the books I read while my son was an infant. Everyone is entitled to their opinion. What is right for one may not be right for another. Knowing your parenting philosophy is helpful, as it helps guide you and gives you grounding upon which to base your decisions in different situations. But you will find that not everyone agrees with the Dr. Karen Parenting Philosophy. At times, you will reprocess your views and check in with yourself to make sure you are doing what works for you, even as you consider the alternatives. Self-checking is healthy as long as you are not changing your parenting style just because someone else disagrees with it if you know what you are doing is right for you and your children.

You will encounter other adults (not just authors) who hold a philosophy that differs from the Dr. Karen Parenting Philosophy.

THE CAMP DIRECTOR EPISODE

The following is the story of the day I returned home after dropping off my six-year-old son at his first day at a new summer camp. I experienced a perfect example of how not only are there people that disagree with the Dr. Karen Parenting Philosophy, but that this philosophy rubs them in such a way that they become defensive, argumentative, and downright nasty.

Here is what happened. Planning for the summer is necessary as early as fall if you want to reserve a spot for your child at the particular summer camp we were considering. We three (my husband, my son, and I) went together so we could evaluate if this camp would be a good fit, or if we should consider one of the other options. When we met with the camp director, we spoke to him and included our son in our discussion. Our son expressed his desire that for the first three days of camp, it would help him feel comfortable and help with his adjustment if one of us could come at lunchtime, give him a quick hug and a kiss, and leave. This would take about ten seconds and help our son feel reassured and adjust to those first three days so he would be able to remain there for the entire summer. We explained to the camp director that he would never have a problem with our son, and that he is very well behaved and participates in everything. He would adjust smoothly. We explained that, simply put, our son has a good understanding of what helps him feel comfortable, and we wanted to follow through with this plan. My husband and I explained clearly that we wanted to help him to feel comfortable. Next, we asked if the director felt comfortable with this plan. Was it okay in terms of his camp philosophy?

This director replied, "I have an open door policy." He added that the parents are "always" the ones with the anxiety and that the children do fine. He then further explained that some parents want to come in and observe their children, but he verbalized that this is a parental issue. "If the child sees the parent at camp," he said, "the child's behavior changes and they do not do as well." We explained that we understood his perspective but in our case, we did not need to observe our son. We explained again that he always does well and adjusts well. Stopping in for a few seconds on those first three days would help him feel confident and reassured. We wanted to find out if this would be okay with the director before we signed up. The director replied that he saw that we were different from other parents who just wanted to observe because of *their own* anxieties. He said he was interested in each child's developmental needs. If that were what our son needed, then it would be fine. Our son said he felt happy that the director would allow us to come and check on him, so we chose to send our son to that camp.

As I think back, perhaps it should have been a red flag for me when the director started to speak about *the other* parents from such a negative perspective. He was really telling us that *we* were anxious and he really did not want us to visit. But at the time, we apparently chose to hear the words that fitted our philosophy and wanted to hear, which included that he was interested in each child's development and that he had an open door policy. I took those words at face value and believed them to be true. I now know that he was lying.

On the first day of summer camp, our son said he wanted one of us to check on him at lunch. We asked him if he really still felt that was needed, and he said it was very important to him. I agreed to check on him, and arrived at lunchtime. I want to take you through my experience, here is what happened. The director yelled that I was not supposed to be coming into the camp as I pleased. I was in shock, as we had agreed I would come.

I reminded the camp director of the discussion that my husband and I had had with him when we were visiting the camp to make our decision. I reminded him that he had agreed that I could come to give my son the comfort he needed. The director responded that he had never said that I could come. But then, a few minutes later, he changed his story and said he had told me to call first if I was going to come. First the director lied and said that he had never said I could come, then he backpedaled and said that he had told me to call first, which clearly implied that he had said I could come. He had never suggested I call first.

I stood in the camp director's office that day and explained what my son needed to feel comfortable. He said if my son was having a good day, then I could not come back tomorrow. I explained to him the issue was not about whether my son was having a good day or not. "I am hopeful and actually assume he will have a great time," I explained. "I really don't think that he won't. I have confidence that he will have a lovely day." The director said, "Since he will be fine, you do not need to come back." This back and forth discussion continued. My point that I verbalized to him was, "It is not about me seeing whether he is fine. It is about my son's adjustment."

Next, the director said that when parents want to observe because they question his camp and his counselors, they can observe from a distance so that the child does not see them. Notice the defensiveness the camp director had.

He further explained that children can be doing fine one moment, and then, when their parent arrives, they are not, it influences them. Thinking back, I remembered his comment about "other parents" in our initial meeting.

I tried to explain my position to him but he clearly could not hear my voice. In my hearing his voice, the director was feeling threatened. He was feeling that I was questioning him, his camp, and his counselors, and therefore he became argumentative. I explained that I was coming for a quick hello because my son said that would help him feel comfortable, but the director could not relate to this. He did not understand it, nor did he try to.

Without my dragging the story on too long, you can clearly see that this director was unable to hear my voice, although, he had heard it when we signed up for the camp and told us what we wanted to hear. I see now that this was his way of getting people into his camp. He led me to think that he agreed with me and understood me, but then once I paid the fee, his tune changed. He said he was going to have to "suffer" two more days of my coming in, and then suffer again when I came to parents' day. During the summer, there is a parent's day where parents are to visit. I must admit that I was surprised at how disrespectful he was. I told him that I was not telling him that his opinion was wrong and mine was right. I said there was a difference between a parent wanting to observe one's child versus a parent that is hearing one's child's needs. In this case, I was listening to my child's voice, thereby considering his needs. This pushed the director over the edge as he then yelled, "You are letting your six-year-old run the show!" Hearing one's child's voice rubs those that do not live by the Dr. Karen Parenting

Philosophy the wrong way.

The level of disrespect shown to me and repeated by his receptionist was the most extreme experience that I had ever encountered. It was an emotionally painful experience. At one point, I said to him that I felt like I was talking to a different man. At our meeting, he had seemed to be compassionate and understanding. He had seemed to consider each child as an individual. Even with my belief that what I was doing was one hundred percent right, this was a painful experience. So, my dear readers, when you experience those in opposition to you, take a deep breath and hold true to your beliefs.

THE GYM CLASS EPISODE

I remember a time when I *was* influenced by an opposing philosophy. Being influenced to do something that you know you should not do often leads to a less than happy ending. Hopefully, we learn from our mistakes. This episode occurred when my son was three years old. Yes, I succumbed to pressure to conform. I learned from that experience that even I need to remind myself to be true to what I believe in; the Dr. Karen Parenting Philosophy.

Here is what happened. I signed my son up for a gymnastics class held at a location he had never been to before. The class was scheduled for one hour a week for eight weeks. I had heard from mothers whose kids were taking gymnastics classes at other locations that you sit and watch, and when I first signed my son up, the registration office had said the parent could stay. When I got there, ready to make myself comfortable, the instructor said I needed to leave and could return when the class was over. I was surprised. I replied that the registration office had told me that parents could stay. He said that perhaps they meant the parent could stay *in the building.* My son was surprised and unprepared for me to leave. In his infinite wisdom, he said, "Mommy, how about this for a plan?" Then he went on to explain his idea. He said he wanted me to stay for his first gym class for the entire hour, at the second class for half an hour, to come back early for the third class, and then for the fourth class and onward I could return at the end of class. That was his personal adjustment plan, which he developed on the spot. In my opinion, his plan was quite appropriate.

The instructor, however, was annoyed by the very idea that my son could negotiate, or even had something to say. The instructor was clearly angry that what *he* said was not immediately obeyed.

It is an important point to note that weeks later, I found out that most classes for his age group at other locations permitted the parents to stay. In fact, I later learned that this same instructor taught the same gym class for three and four-year-olds in a different location where the parents sat and watched the entire time. Thus, the idea of the parents leaving was his preference because that is what he personally liked, his personal philosophy, having nothing to do with a policy of the program or about the development of the children.

When the gym teacher said that no parents were allowed to stay, I explained that my son's idea would help him to succeed in the class. The instructor replied, "Your son will be fine. You need to leave. If you need to observe, you can do that from somewhere he does not see you." I explained that it was not that *I needed* to observe, but that my son needed to see that I was there.

This instructor felt his ability was being questioned. I recognize that this instructor's mentality was the same as the camp director's. They both hold a belief system that needing to observe is a parental issue. They believe that children do not and should not have a voice. At the time, I must admit, I felt pressure. The other parents all left because the "boss" said so. Some kids were crying, some were content, some were happy, and others looked very nervous and hesitant rather than excited to be there. I talked with my son and told him I was going to leave. I told him where I would be waiting. Needless to say, he was so concerned about my not being there that he did not enjoy the class. He spent a good deal of his class time trying to hold his tears back, but he finally started crying. So what happened? The instructor had to come and get me. He also said, sounding very annoyed, that I might as well just stay next time.

The following week, my son did not want to return. He verbalized his discomfort in not feeling safe in the class since his voice was not being heard by the instructor. How could I blame him? He was right not to return. The instructor really did not care about my son's opinion, his voice. He was actually disrespectful to my son. Just because he is a young child does not mean he should not be treated with respect, according to the Dr. Karen Parenting Philosophy. How could he trust this instructor to help him with his physical needs (e.g., the high bar), when he proved to not be available for his emotional needs? As humans, we learn to trust through saying how we feel and observing whether another hears us. When another person pushes our voice to the side, which shows us that we do not really matter to them, it makes us feel like they are not looking out for us.

Would you marry someone who says no when you say you need help with a problem? Imagine a wife saying to her husband, "I feel really sad when you ignore me when you come home from work. I understand if you need some time to yourself after a long day, but could you at least say hello back to me when I say hello? Perhaps we can give each other a quick hug, and then you can go take the time you need." Now imagine the husband answering, "No, I won't say hello, and I certainly won't give you a hug. I feel what you need is to have your voice ignored." Clearly, my son chose not to "marry" this gym teacher. When he realized that his voice was not being heard, he did not return to that class.

The following year, when I was planning on signing my son up for a sports club, I checked into its reputation by asking around. Many parents said it had an excellent reputation. The class met once a week. In advance of signing up, I talked with my son about the program. This program did require parents to leave. I knew this before signing him up. I worked with my son to create a plan together, in advance, that he felt comfortable with. The plan was that during the first class, I would stay in the waiting area, the second class in the car, and by the third class, he would be all set. When the coach saw me in the waiting area, he suggested that I leave the building because kids do better when they know their parents are not there. I replied that in order for the sports club to work for my son, I would be in the waiting area the first day, in my car the second day, and after that I would leave. This coach looked at me in such a way that I recognized that he disagreed with my opinion, but rather than this becoming a conflict, he was actually respectful of my voice and simply let the situation be. I had learned from my past experience that I must apply my own philosophy. I also recognized at that moment that my son had a coach that would be great, as he had his opinions, but was open to others. My son was extremely successful there and has been attending that sports club every year since then without me being there. It was just the first time that he needed the adjustment plan.

A few weeks after the first class, the coach approached me and told me that he was sorry that he may have seemed annoyed at the first class, and that typically, when parents hung around, it affected how the children acted in a negative way. He explained that this was clearly not the case with my son. I replied that each child is different and that I appreciated his being open to our plan, even though he disagreed with it. Now this is a coach that you want for your child; one that holds the perspective of hearing another's voice.

THE DENTIST EPISODE

At age six and a half, my son got his first cavity. I was told that due to the style of that particular tooth (e.g., the grooves), it made sense that he got a cavity in that tooth. Therefore, explained the dentist, I should not blame myself nor should my son feel bad about his brushing style. As the parent, I felt I was to blame, of course, although the statement from the dentist was mildly reassuring. I digress though, as this is not the point of the story. The point goes back to the challenges you may face.

I asked the dentist if he had any literature and/or would be kind enough to take a moment to explain the tooth-filling procedure to my son, as he does better when he knows what to expect in advance. The dentist said he did not have time right now and would explain it on the day of the appointment. That should have told me right off the bat that having my son go to the dentist that my husband and I go to rather than a pediatric dentist was a mistake. He was familiar with our dentist because he had occasionally gone with my husband or me to our appointments. The dentist is extremely skilled in his dental abilities, and great in his behavior with adults. In addition, his staff is efficient and kind, so it just made sense to have him go there. I soon learned that I should have listened to my inner voice about what my son needed; i.e., detailed information about what to expect, which is what is provided at a pediatric dentist office if so desired.

On the day of the appointment, the dentist showed my son the equipment and explained the procedure. As I had predicted, my son became very uncomfortable seeing all the equipment on the day of the appointment instead of beforehand. My son wanted to take the time to understand what each piece of equipment was for, and needed time to process it. It was evident that the dentist's patience was wearing thin as his eyebrows clenched and he looked at his watch. What I saw was that the dentist did not consider a child as a person to spend time on. He did not hear my voice or my son's voice. He had his opinion and was going to do what he thought, regardless of what we might say.

After about five minutes, the dentist became quite frustrated and told my son it was time to begin. My son started crying and said, "I need time to understand about all of the equipment." The dentist leaned close to my son and told him, "Stop crying. It is time to do the procedure. Other people are waiting." My son was trying to hold his tears in. He said; "I am trying to be brave, but I am scared." I spoke with him and he started to calm down and feel better.

Then, as the dentist was about to begin, the dentist exacerbated the situation by giving my son a warning. "Now remember, no crying or your mommy won't be allowed to stay in the room." A tear rolled down my son's face. The dentist put his hand on my son's face and tapped it and repeated, "No crying, I said, or your mommy will have to leave the room." My son was ready to have the cavity filled once I helped to calm him down, but the dentist threatened him not once but twice. I explained to the dentist that threats do not work with my son. I then started to talk with my son again, and as he started to calm down, I knew he would be fine. We were already there, and I knew the dentist was skillful, so I thought if I could just work with my son, we could get through this and switch to a pediatric dentist for all future appointments. The problem was that the dentist was not working with me or my son. As my son started to calm down again, the dentist said, "Quiet, Mom. It is always the mother that is more nervous than the child."

This situation is a similar theme to those of the camp director and the gymnastics class. The person "in charge" does not agree that we should hear the child's voice. The person "in charge" does not agree with the Dr. Karen Parenting Philosophy.

Instead of hearing my voice, the dentist stuck with his pre-existing belief system. There are people who lump all children together and decide they are going to handle all situations with all children all the same way. As I tried to verbalize what worked with my son, and it was obvious that when I spoke to my son he did calm down, it became abundantly clear that the dentist had the old-school type philosophy where children are to be seen and not heard. Any type of behavior on the part of a parent that steers away from that philosophy was a challenge, to him. We signed up with a pediatric dentist after that experience. We are all on a journey of learning from our experiences, are we not?

Common Challenges

The following are a few of the common challenges you may face.

OTHERS IN YOUR CIRCLE DISAGREE

If you have read this book and your spouse has not, and you both typically parent in different ways, then my philosophy may make you feel like your spouse is making it more challenging for you to implement your newfound knowledge. If you take this concept further, and your spouse is not as open to trying this philosophy, as his philosophy appears to be glued to him, you may feel like your attempts are for nothing, as you cannot over-power him. You feel like you are spinning your wheels. My suggestions about how to handle this common problem when others in your circle disagree with your methodology are as follows:

What not to do:

Do not say, "I am right and you are wrong."

What to do:

Discuss with this person that it is not that you feel your view is right and his is wrong, but simply that your view works for you. Say that you feel this concept will work and hope that he might be willing to try it. Ask him if he could at least give you a chance to explain the philosophy and talk about it, rather than engage in a battle of who is right and who is wrong.

What not to do:

Do not imply and assume. For example, do not just leave this book on the table, implying that you want him to read it. Do not assume that he will read it. He may or may not notice it, and his actions or lack thereof will cause you to react.

What to do:

Tell him you have noticed that you and he have experienced certain challenges as a parenting team, and that you want to explore with him some ideas that you can both work on as a parenting team to help your family and your children as individuals become more successful. During your conversation, tell him that you have investigated some books to help. Say that you understand that you may have some similar opinions and some different ones to his.

Verbalize that there is a book with a philosophy you think would be useful, even though it is different from what he has been doing. State that you are curious about experimenting with the new ideas and are wondering if he saw the same problems that you have noticed about your children's behaviors, and whether he finds those behaviors as challenging as you do. Ask if he would like to join you in trying a different approach.

OTHER CHILDREN QUESTION YOUR ACTIONS

As discussed, spending quality time with your children is one of the nine key techniques of implementing the Dr. Karen Parenting Philosophy. I recall playing baseball in our front yard with my son when he was five. A four-year-old neighbor asked, "Why are you playing with Jeremy?" At the young age of four, she questioned this play, as though it was odd for me to be playing with my son. Is it so unheard of to play, I mean really play, with your child?

OTHER PARENTS QUESTION YOUR ACTIONS AND RAISE THEIR EYEBROWS AT YOU

My husband often has the opportunity to attend a football game or play golf on the weekend with friends/colleagues. Although he will occasionally join in, his typical response is that unless the invitation includes his son, since it is on the weekend, he really cannot accept. Some may question his reply or raise their eyebrows at this. I must say that I think my husband's choice to pick and choose how often, when, and where he goes, and being considerate of father-son play and family time is great. He feels that our son would love to participate in certain activities, and it would not be fair to him to be away the whole day on a weekend after being at work all week. My husband takes certain time on some weekends for personal time. But he also enjoys quality time at the weekend with his son. The balance of personal and father-son time is important. Many times, the person inviting my husband somewhere says he would not do that for *his* child. Other times, the person has no children and finds it odd that my husband would put his child first.

There are times when there are others you meet that value this philosophy and parenting choice, so I shall briefly mention this, although the focus of this chapter is on the challenges you may face. For an example, I recall a lovely example when my husband's friend had extra baseball tickets. My husband communicated that he would love to spend the weekend time with his son and perhaps the dads could bring their sons. The gentleman that had the tickets responded that he never would have thought of making it a father-son outing. He then verbalized that it was a great idea. The fathers and sons had a great day at the game.

There are also adults that do not have children of their own, but agree with and value my husband's philosophy. I recall one friend of my husband's in particular who made it clear that when the time comes and he also has a child, he will be quite an involved father. His parenting philosophy of being a true active participant in a child's life is there even prior to this man having children of his own.

Spending time with their children is a beautiful thing for parents to do. When we are blessed with children, more parents should relish their time with their children. In fact, we should be spending more time with our children. Each child deserves our attention. I am here to remind you that the years go by fast, so enjoy your relationship with your children now, and do activities that they enjoy. It is fun for your kids and fun for you. The time you spend with your children affects your relationship in the present and the future, as well as impacts who they become both in the short run and in the long run.

Another example of other parents questioning your actions and raising their eyebrows at you includes the example I discussed in Chapter 3 of when my young son was not ready to have a play date at a girl's house without me being there. At the time, the mother said that unless he could come without me, he was not welcome into her home. Her parenting philosophy is clearly different from mine. An important point of the Dr. Karen Parenting Philosophy that the choices we make today do indeed impact the development of our children shines through in this example. Two years later, my son and this girl were at a birthday party and an interesting incident arose. My son gave me a hug and a kiss and asked me to return toward the end of the party when it was cake time. The little girl did not want her mother to leave and kept clinging to her. This is a clear example of how children develop confidence and comfort if their voices are heard. My dear readers, this is an example to remind you to stay true to the Dr. Karen Parenting Philosophy.

OTHER CHILDREN'S BEHAVIOR

Having respectful and responsible children does not mean that other children will behave in a respectful and responsible manner. This very fact is another common challenge you may face. Ideally, all children will be respectful and responsible to one another, but sadly, this is not always the case. Thus, it is important to help your child when he encounters situations where others are not acting in a manner he considers appropriate. He needs to learn that he cannot make another child be respectful and responsible.

Respectful and responsible children may feel emotionally pained when they see other children acting disrespectfully or irresponsibly. As parents, we need to help our child cope positively with the fact that others will not always be respectful and responsible.

A key notion to help your children is the idea that we cannot control the thoughts and behaviors of others, only our own.

The following are examples:

Picture your fourteen-year-old daughter, who is respectful and responsible. A new girl enters her class. The other kids ignore her because she is new. In contrast, your daughter talks with her and says, "Hi. Do you know we have a drama club? I am part of this club and if you like drama, I am sure if we spoke to the teacher in charge even though it is a few months into the school year, maybe you can get in." The new girl replies, "Do I look like I would want to join the drama club?"

Just because your child is respectful and trying to act in

170

a responsible manner by trying in her own way to welcome this new girl, it does not necessarily mean the other person will respond respectfully. Your fourteen-year-old tried to be responsible about what is happening in her classroom. She tried to be respectful of the new girl by paying attention to her rather than ignoring her. From your daughter's position, the new girl was quite dismissive and rude.

Picture another scenario where your sixteen-year-old daughter is asked on a date. The boy, named Brett, shows up at her house at the time they had decided upon. Your daughter nicely tells him she is almost ready, she just needs about five more minutes to finish her makeup. Brett says, "If you are not ready in one minute, I am out of here." There are a variety of different ways a person who has respect for herself might respond in contrast to a person that does not have respect for his own self. A girl who respects herself may say something along the lines of, "Sorry I am a few minutes late, I hope you can be patient. Are you serious? You will leave? Seriously?" And perhaps she may laugh a little, then add, "It won't take me long. Come in and relax. I'm worth the wait, aren't I?" Or she might say, "If you really can't wait five minutes for me, then I guess you really don't want to go out with me, after all. Is that true, or would you like to wait?" She might also say, "That was kind of rude. You really won't wait?" Or she may say something like, "Are you just wanting me to know how important it is that we leave when you want to? Because all you need to do is let me know how you feel. You don't have to threaten to leave." In contrast, if she does not respect herself, she may just instantly go with him without saying a word, or just say, "I'm sorry."

Of course, one could argue that she was not being respectful of him or responsible by being late. There is truth to that. Does one then continue in that frame where he should then be disrespectful to her, and then she would be disrespectful in her further communications to him, and then him right back at her? Every moment is an opportunity to act in a respectful manner to yourself and to another and make responsible choices.

Picture another scenario where your nine-year-old son tells you that another boy at camp cries whenever anyone says something mean to him, or when he falls during a sports event. Many of the other boys call him a crybaby. Your son says it is very mean of the other boys to say that, and he would never say that. Your child may very well observe others being mean and disrespectful to each other. It will seem odd and not make sense to him that other children would do that when he would never even consider doing it. It is your job to help your child find how he can experience this part of his life in such a way that he remains respectful and responsible even when others are not, and how he can still be emotionally okay. He can learn how to listen to his inner voice about how to handle such situations.

Picture another scenario where your ten-year-old tells you that a girl she thought was her friend was whispering about her with two other girls, and it really hurt her feelings. She then says it makes her want to do something mean back to the girl to hurt her feelings, but she is not going to. Your daughter continues to say that just because someone else is disrespectful, it does not mean she should be. What a lovely example! A ten-year-old remains respectful and responsible and finds it within herself how to feel good about her decision.

There are so many moments on any given day with children of any age group where a child who is respectful and responsible may encounter a situation where another child is not being respectful and responsible. Picture another scenario where your two-year-old son is at a children's museum with you. There is a section in the museum that is roped off for children younger than four to play, where they can climb up a ladder, and then slide down a slide. From my point of view, this is an environment where parents do need to be on top of what is going on, as this is a wonderful opportunity to help young children learn respectful and responsible interactions with other children.

You watch a few of the children pushing and cutting in front of other children, making it difficult for the more polite children to have a chance to climb or slide. If you taught your two-year-old to be respectful and wait his turn, the children that have not learned the same lesson cut in front of him. Perhaps there is a child who even pushes him out of the line. As the parent, you have many options. The following are just some ideas a parent might think of:

a.   Come back later when those kids are not there. (There is always going to be a disrespectful child, so the odds are if you come back later, it will be a different child doing the same and/or similar behavior).

b.   Gently ask the few children who are cutting to please wait their turn so that everyone can have a chance.

c.   Take charge and stand right there, saying, "You are

next. Wait your turn. Okay, now you can go." You direct the traffic.

d. Ask the parents of the children that are cutting if they can help so all of the kids have a turn. (You notice that the parents of the misbehaving disrespectful children are not paying attention to their children's behavior. They are either on their cell phone, reading a magazine, or chatting with their friends).

e. Stand in such a way that you are blocking the children from cutting in front of your child. Once he gets up the ladder, you can back away and let the others go.

f. Teach your child what he can say to the other children to help him try to solve the problem.

g. Say and do nothing and let your child and the other respectful ones suffer.

Among the variety of choices, some are higher on the "yes" scale than others. The point right now is not to consider what you would actually do, or even add a few choices of your own, but rather to consider that it can be tough for the parent of the respectful child to witness rudeness toward your own child. The experience can be tough for your child, too. It is hard for the respectful child to experience such disrespect. As this child grows up, he will continue to experience episodes when others are disrespectful. It may disappoint him that there are others in the world who are not as respectful or responsible as he is. With your help, he will learn how to cope with and respond in those situations. He will gravitate towards other children who possess the core character of respect and responsibility.

Whether your child is witnessing disrespectful and/or irresponsible behavior, or he experiences another child aiming such behavior at him, it is hard for the respectful child because he finds himself spending time thinking about it. He may spend time processing the event because it does not fit with who he is. That is a challenge. Your child may tell you about what occurred and what he is processing. He may look to you for answers. It becomes a challenge for you.

Would you rather raise a disrespectful and irresponsible child who becomes a disrespectful and irresponsible adult, or would you rather raise a respectful and responsible child who becomes a respectful and responsible adult? Do you still want the latter, even though it means that there will be challenges?

What to do:

As discussed above, children that are respectful and responsible will encounter others who are not, from time to time. What you can do, what would be quite helpful, is if you discuss such situations. Let your child know she can always come and talk to you. Explain to your child that it may be disappointing when others are not meeting up to her standards. As mentioned previously in this chapter, explain to your child that we cannot control the behavior of others, only our own. You can even go so far as providing your child with an example of where observing another person's disrespectful behavior in one context may or may not mean that person acts that way in another context. Explore with your child it is always a choice to spend more or less time with a person.

For an example, consider a situation where your daughter has discussed with you her friendship with a girl named Sally from school. Your daughter explains to you that when she asks Sally to please pass the markers, Sally consistently does not. She keeps them all for herself. This is disrespectful. Your child also noticed that when she is playing sports with Sally, she is great fun and passes the ball to her. Your child learns that with this classmate she may consider gravitating more toward her when it comes to sports than in art work.

Or you can certainly teach your daughter that her style of communication may impact the behavior of others, but in the end, as previously discussed, you cannot control others. For an example, when your daughter says, "Come on, Sally, let's take turns. It is such a nice thing to do, and I appreciate it," Sally typically shares. But when your daughter just hollers, "Sally!" Sally just ignores her. You can explore this with your child. Therefore, you may explain to her that she may be acting in a respectful manner in her request to Sally to share the markers, but Sally may still be disrespectful. Tell your child that she knows how to behave in such a way that makes her feel good inside. That is the key. Tell her you are proud of her and hope that she takes pride in herself.

There are challenges we must face in our life. The challenges you may face with some people when incorporating the Dr. Karen Parenting Philosophy is well worth it.

CHAPTER 13

FINAL THOUGHTS

The Dr. Karen Parenting Philosophy may be controversial. My goal is to teach families that are looking for answers what I believe works in raising respectful children that make responsible choices. I am interested in arming parents with the knowledge I have. Why keep this all to myself? Why not share it? I am the leading authority on the Dr. Karen Parenting Philosophy and the nine key techniques that make the philosophy work. It is not just a theory. It is a theory with action.

There are some parents who do not want to take the time, or make an effort to make personal and family shifts, even though they say they want things to improve in their family. It is those parents that want to improve their children's behavior, but they want a magic wand, a quick fix. They want someone else to solve the problem. Your child's teacher cannot change your child's behavior, your child's doctor cannot, nor can your child's therapist. Merely *telling* your child to be respectful and responsible will not make it happen, either. As the parent, you must do more. It is up to parents to help their children develop true respect for self and others, and therefore act respectfully and display responsible behavior.

Bringing helping agents into your child's life (e.g., therapist) cannot do the work for you. It is the agents that can help you to help yourself, help you to help your children, and help your child to help himself. It is your job to do the work outside of the appointment to implement what the agent has helped you with. It is your job to help your children to help themselves, as the agent cannot do this without you, as parents are the key players in their children's lives.

There are parents who are ready and willing to do what it takes to help their children become more respectful and responsible. There are also adults who have recently become parents and long to learn how to raise respectful children, and they recognize the power of incorporating a parenting philosophy in the child's early years, and continuing it as the child grows. There are parents who resonate with the Dr. Karen Parenting Philosophy, but want validation, enhancement, and tips. This book is for you, any of the scenarios of parents listed, as well as for any parent scenario not mentioned.

Through the years, there have been books that blame parents for their children's behaviors. There are books that counter that philosophy, and support the notion that children are born with their own temperament, which parents cannot control. I am here to say that both philosophies hold truth. Children are born with their own temperaments. There are things that are not in a parent's control. At the same time, children are very much influenced by the experiences they have. As parents, we are a significant part of our child's environment.

It is not a debate between nature or nurture, genetics or environment as to which influences our children to be who they are. It simply is not a debate because this is not an either/or concept; it is a both/and concept. Our children are made up of their biology and their experiences. We play a great role in our children's development, on who they become. To think otherwise is giving yourself a get-out-of-parenting-free card. That card typically has the tendency to bite you and your children in the butt.

It is this author's whole-hearted contention that as parents, we can ease, exacerbate, and/or enhance a pre-existing personality trait or inborn temperament. In essence, we can help our children become all that they can be. We do have an influence. I have often heard parents say that my techniques are magical. Parents have told me that they cannot believe how quickly they see actual changes when they implement the Dr. Karen Parenting Philosophy. You also have the opportunity to potentially see shifts rather quickly. You have to work hard for what you want in life. You must do the work in parenting, too. You must apply the nine techniques with consistency if you want to see both short-term and long-term results. What you put into your life plays a role in what you and those you love get out of life. Is life perfect? No, it is not. Your children are not going to meet your standards every second of every day. Can children learn from parents how to be respectful and responsible? The answer is yes, absolutely, indeed.

There are many families that want to enhance their world, and are motivated to do the work to achieve enhancement. There are others that do not do the work and remain stagnant or decline. The Dr. Karen Parenting Philosophy and the nine techniques discussed in this book have touched many, and helped many families help themselves get to a better place. Truly positive, life-long shifts have occurred. As a clinician and as a human being, I feel touched and honored to have played a role and continue to play a role in people's lives to help them be happier. I did not write this book to make friends or enemies. I wrote this book to touch people who are ready to be touched, for parents who are interested in a most exciting journey of family harmony and the development of respectful and responsible children. For parents who want a parenting concept, along with concrete guidance on how to get there, this is who this book is written for.

The parent-child relationship has the potential to be beautiful. Children have the potential to be responsible and respectful here and now and on into the future if they are simply given the tools. For those who are ready to help their child become respectful and be responsible, I am excited that you are ready to take on this journey. And for you who are not sure, I am cheering for you, too. My thoughts are with you and your loved ones. Consider the philosophy, consider the techniques. Explore them, experiment with them, and discuss this book and your thoughts about it with those you are closest to on your journey.

You can make a positive difference in the lives of your family.

Best wishes to my readers for happiness and family harmony, coming from me to you with all sincerity. I am cheering for you.

Dr. Karen Ruskin

REFERENCES

Bateson, G. (1972). *Steps to an Ecology of Mind.* New York: Chandler Publishing Company.

O'Hanlon, B., & Wilk, J. (1987). *Shifting Contexts.* New York: Guilford Press.